Living in the Lowlands

D1535642

Living in the Lowlands
The Dutch Domestic Scene 1850-2004

Netherlands Architecture Institute, Rotterdam
NAi Publishers, Rotterdam

Introduction
Just Housing

The Beauty of Dutch Residential Architecture

The beauty of building in this country resides in its rows of narrow houses together figuring a city of complexity and clarity, its blocks of flats marching towards a better world, its hybrid geometries knitting together the existing fabric and its collages of intersecting planes reconfiguring social relations. Not palaces or office buildings, not opera houses or memorials, but the collective lived reality inhabited every day by its residents is what determines the character and the distinctive look of the Netherlands. The attraction of its built spaces comes from the clarity of these formal devices, not from their ability to amaze us with their scale, their richness or their strangeness. Their very everyday simplicity gives them a sense of rightness that produces a particularly Dutch form of beauty.

The Netherlands Architecture Institute collects, preserves, examines and makes available the documents that tell the story of this residential environment. The archives of Dutch architecture since the beginning of the nineteenth century are housed here, and exhibitions, publications and discussions make use of these collections to show how the Netherlands has developed a manner of building homes that is both collective and highly varied in its parts, pieces and permutations. This book, which accompanies a selected display of the Institute's permanent collection, summarizes that narrative. Instead of offering a historical overview, it concentrates on what Dutch architecture produces at its best, which is the domestic environment. By showing the beauty of what has been built, it argues for an architecture that provides a material, visually disciplined framework in which social and political life is lived, understood and changed.

Dutch architecture is housing

Any selection of good Dutch architecture is of necessity marked by a preponderance of housing projects. Taken together, these buildings also give a coherent, although not stylistically unified, picture of the distinct manner of making residential forms here. The architecture of this country distinguishes itself from most of its neighbours exactly in its focus on such structures, but also in the way in which it has developed housing types. These are not, on the whole, single-family detached homes or villas, but communal structures: originally (from the late fifteenth century on) rows of brick façades whose windows become larger and larger over time, but later also apartment blocks arranged in abstract compositions, as well as monumental urban patterns produced by the modulation of either the brick walls or the disposition of the housing blocks.

Outside the Netherlands, architecture is more resolutely, as it has been since Vitruvius (who aimed to serve the state by producing, most importantly, defensive structures) and especially since the founding of the Académie des Beaux-Arts in 1648, the built affirmation of social, economic and political power. In this tradition, architecture was defined as a profession precisely to accommodate the needs of the central state for buildings that would represent as well as house it. Lesser types, such as housing, factories or, later, commercial buildings, were not accepted as architecture until the middle of the nineteenth century, and then tended to clothe themselves in the cloaks tailored originally for Beaux-Arts monuments. Architectural experimentation usually took place outside of this canon, either in 'less important' buildings or in utopian projects and, increasingly, in single-family homes. In these neighbouring countries, architecture remained the mask of money and power. There it still resides in the places where power accumulates itself into physical property and luxury, or is exercised, whether this is in palaces or churches or, more recently, office buildings and private homes. The 'purest' architecture often takes place where power appears nakedly, as in bunkers and treasuries; where it is memorialized through monuments to great men and deeds; where it is sublimated into the luxurious enjoyment of its fruits, as in cultural institutions; or where it draws its subjects into it to be educated or enlightened according to the standards it sets.

Not in the Netherlands. Here housing, and especially public-sector housing, is what has mattered for the way in which the built environment appears. Though there are certainly monumental buildings here, they are in general not the structures by which Dutch architecture distinguishes itself. They often seem, in fact, to be out of place, as the famous Palace on the Dam, or like overwrought experiments in adapting foreign aesthetics to the Dutch situation, as in the new ING Bank Headquarters in Amsterdam. What is different here are the rows of houses along the canals, the Amsterdam School housing blocks, the 'white villages' of J.J.P. Oud, the new town of Almere, and the recent experiments in Borneo-Sporenburg, Leidsche Rijn and Ypenburg. This is housing that never builds up into massive blocks, nor falls apart into individual blocks expressing only the dreams of one occupant. It is housing that is tight and often quite small, but that together aspires to a greater sense of a place inhabited collectively.

There are concrete historic and physical reasons for this situation. Some of them are very basic. The soil of the historic Dutch heartland, the area north and west of the Rhine delta, is so soft as to make the construction of large structures extremely difficult. Settlement patterns on this land were based on the presence of dams, dykes, sheltered ports and other water-based infrastructural focal points, rather than castles and fortifications (which did occur in the less-populated eastern and southern part of the country), large marketplaces, or other natural characteristics. This meant that the reason for the town's existence was often invisible, leaving it to the houses to define the urban areas' character. The reclamation of land also established a geometry of polders and irrigation ditches, canals and locks that was replicated in urban configurations as towns grew. The political structure that developed partially as the result of this condition was non-hierarchical and diffused, built up out of cooperative guilds and competing commercial interests, small landholdings and associations formed to manage water and create polders. There were few grand rulers and little native display of power.

Building on this condition, the Dutch very early on developed methods of urban planning and preservation that differed from those in neighbouring countries. The most famous of these is the plan for the expansion of Amsterdam of 1648, which, as Ed Taverne famously pointed out in his seminal *In 't land van belofte; in de nieue stadt: Ideaal en werkelijkheid van de stadsuitleg in de Republiek 1580-1680* of 1978, was the first example of public-private real estate speculation. The establishment of plot plans based on infrastructure and existing settlement patterns, the institution of detailed zoning and building regulations, and the subsequent freedom left each buyer to create, with prevalent building methods and materials, his own home, allowed for the emergence of a unified, and yet subtly varied domestic scene. This environment was subsequently lovingly pictured and preserved, sometimes, as in the case of the painter and fire-prevention expert Jan van der Heyden, by the same person.

The 'canal belt' remains the *locus classicus* of Dutch housing, not least because the physical results were so well suited to its environment. The collective wall was modulated up by the continual turning of the canals, creating a more intimate and non-hierarchical geometry, and its uniform brick façades broken up by the large expanses of glass. The narrow configuration of the houses' interiors was also perfected to such a degree that the amount of development since then has been relatively minor. There is a sense of logical and continuous harmony about this scene that Dutch architects and their clients have sought to replicate ever since, and that now has also become a popular model for urban development in countries as far away as China, where several imitation Dutch cities, designed by firms such as Kuipers Compagnons, are now under construction.

For several centuries, this was almost all the Netherlands offered to architecture. The real innovations in housing after the Golden Age took place elsewhere, and until the late nineteenth century this country contributed little to the emergence of the terrace house, the suburban cottage development, the 'mietskaserne' or the 'city palace.' The passage of the Housing Act of 1901, however, marked a distinct change in this situation. Under the leadership of the social democratic movement, it sought to legislate the right to decent housing for all Dutch citizens. Because of the complex Dutch political relations, in which Protestant, Catholic, and Liberal balanced each other so completely that no single ideology or model for communal form-making could dominate, however, this collective determinism was bound to a legal structure in which the actual construction of housing would be led by private and semi-private corporations. This gave rise to the emergence of the collective housing associations representing various social groups, but the law also codified the tradition of public involvement with urban expansion in cooperation with such (semi-) private groups. Thus backward-looking images of communal form (favoured by Catholics), as well as rational, open structures favoured by Liberals and later Social Democrats, and the hybrid designs combining rural and urban forms favoured by Protestant groups, could all be realized under the aegis of corporations set up by the different groups. What remained was a neutral, but also connective role for the government. Urban planning as it was practised by city bureaucracies was here not just a question of laying down abstract zoning regulations but, as it was worked out in detail in the realization of H.P. Berlage's Plan Zuid in Amsterdam, a matter of defining the three-dimensional character of the building blocks and surrounding public spaces in order to produce a coherence along with a great deal of variety and freedom for different groups to apply their signatures to the city.

Though the aesthetic and planning methodologies developed originally by cities such as Amsterdam after passage of the 1901 law sought to adapt existing patterns to meet new social demands and utilize new technologies, a split soon developed between those who called for a more radical break with existing conditions and those who wished to resurrect an often rurally tinged ideal at the edges of the fast-growing cities. Much has been made in Dutch architectural history of this split between modernist and traditionalist forms, such as the aggressive abstractions produced by Berlage in Amsterdam and later Van den Broek en Bakema in Rotterdam versus the almost extruded farmhouse-like forms favoured by Granpré Molière in cities like Breda, but what is most remarkable, when one views these structures from a distance, is the degree to which these two tendencies became intertwined in the work of architects such as Oud and Dudok, and in cities such as Rotterdam. Dudok's work combined

Wrightian composition with shed roofs that appear 'traditional' in the Dutch context, Oud produced both 'the White City' and neo-classical buildings, and Rotterdam was largely rebuilt after the Second World War with housing blocks that combine aggressive and large-scale urban forms with neo-classical details. Partially this was the result of the adoption of the originally German idea of 'raumplannung' ('ruimtelijke ordening') or spatial arrangement, in which planning was seen as a continual and dynamic process involving all stakeholders in a negotiated three-dimensional rearrangement of the physical environment.

The emergence of effective methods of mass production after the Second World War, as well as the need for a radical expansion of the existing housing stock, caused clearer distinctions between opposing tendencies to appear. The adaptation of various concrete prefabrication modules, the move out of the core city to open meadows taken over in their entirety for new neighbourhoods, and the desire to make a place with and within such conditions, led to sharply contrasting experiments. Whereas the path chosen by different housing authorities was originally defined by political and religious motives, with Catholicism becoming associated with traditional architecture, by the 1960s it was a question of one's attitude toward the place of housing: should it be an efficient and scientific appropriation of space, or a human-scaled and ad hoc development of place? Both approaches were tried at various times and at various places, and sometimes, as in Almere or on the eastern edges of Rotterdam, simultaneously. Since then, optimistic applications of large-scale technologically based solutions have gone in and out of favour, as have more small-scale, recognizable housing forms.

What continues to distinguish Dutch residential architecture is its anti-monumental, collective and modular quality. From the brick façades left uncovered, so that the module of construction is clearly visible, to the prefabrication window, door and sill combinations plugged into clearly distinguishable concrete frames; from the complex 'stamps' out of which housing blocks, neighbourhoods and whole cities were built up in the 1960s, to the octagonal fragments surrounding 'living yards' in the 'cabbage architecture' of the 1970s; from the resurrection of the canal house as a modernist collage by West 8 to the adaptation of Berlage's collective city form by T. Koolhaas in Almere, there is a sense in Dutch domestic architecture that the whole and the parts are in an unstable, but clearly visible relationship with each other. Dutch residential architecture is self-referential, enclosed and enclosing, creating a highly habitable artificial environment. Henry James noted it about Amsterdam when he visited in 1900: it was a 'harmonious' place, 'striking no chords that lead elsewhere.'

As such, Dutch housing represents the 'polder model,' not only as a physical form, but as a political phenomenon as well. The dams, canals, meadows and irrigation ditches continue to be specified into urban form whose materialization is an appropriate, but distinct, variation on the underlying pattern, while the whole is also the result of complex negotiations and investments by multiple parties (state and city government, building corporations, and buyers), thus reflecting a resolutely anti-hierarchical social structure. It is also a result that is not stable: Dutch housing is not built for the ages, but is continually renovated, reused, torn down, adapted and rebuilt as norms and values change. Built on artificial territory that is too precious to be wasted, it is a commodity that has to adapt itself to changing social, economic and physical conditions.

This last characteristic, derived from the open-ended quality of the building process and the social structure commissioning that construction, carried out by parsimonious investment in a modular built form, and evaluated in a culture that has no clear ideology, is what in the end defines Dutch housing.

The NAI's architecture collection

The Netherlands Architecture Institute houses a unique collection of architectural drawings, sketches, collages and photographs, which documents the story of this Dutch housing.

Within the scope of numerous existing collections, the NAI collection occupies a special place. Special because it is not limited to the best works, as in many other collections, but contains the complete archives of an extensive group of architects, not just the most well-known. Special also because this collection is anchored in an institute with a broad set of objectives, allowing it to serve as a source of inspiration and a base for countless activities in the opportunities it offers for researching and presenting material.

The history of the creation of the NAI collection dates back to the second half of the nineteenth century, when the architecture community began collecting architectural drawings and publishing journals featuring modern designs as well as assessments of older buildings. By the beginning of the twentieth century, the architects realized the importance of preserving their work and sought to establish an architecture museum in order to create a memoir of Dutch architecture, as well as underscore the significance of individual designs. 'It is simply easier for a young poet to find a publisher than for a young architect to find a patron. Consequently many architectural ideas remain confined to paper (…). For the development of architecture, the study of ideals is far more important than that of completed buildings' (J.H.W. Leliman, 'Een architectuurmuseum', *De Opmerker* 11 (1912), pp. 345-347). In addition, architects considered an important task of such a museum to be publicizing Dutch architecture and related arts by organizing exhibitions in the Netherlands and abroad. Only in the 1970s would genuine steps be undertaken, including by the government, to establish an architecture museum. And it would only become a reality after 1993, in a newly designed building, as the Netherlands Architecture Institute.

An architect's originality and wealth of ideas only become clear once the context of the design and the environment in which it operates are examined. To make this possible, the NAI has from the very beginning set out to collect complete archives. The collection features a wide variety of designers and designs; it contains material not only by internationally renowned architects such as Berlage, Oud and Rem Koolhaas, but also by highly gifted designers who have not (yet) achieved great fame. In addition, the collection is characterized by great diversity: from sketch to working drawing, from maquette to personal correspondence, from photograph to computer-aided design.

The core of the NAI collection is clearly the archives of architects who were significant in the developments of housing construction, in part because the far-reaching impact housing construction has had on the development of architecture in the Netherlands. The field of work of architecture is currently extending into other disciplines, and this is reflected in the collection. Urban planning has always been part of the acquisitions policy, but landscape architecture, interiors and to a certain extent design itself, an essential component of the current forms of the conceptual process, are now included in the collection as well.

Of course, a collection derives its significance from the way it is put to use. And this use of the collection at the NAI continually changes. Researchers and users, moreover, contribute new meanings through the approaches they select. For many years, the NAI collection was primarily the subject of research into architectural history. At certain times, the focus was on research into monographs and styles; in other periods, thematic, technical, philosophical or theoretical research predominated. In recent years, analysis of buildings based on the NAI collection has become part of design courses, and history is being used as a source of inspiration for individual design. The NAI collection is not static – on the contrary, just as architecture changes, the collection changes and evolves along with it. It invites use, offers room for all conceivable approaches and in turn derives its own benefit from this. Documents are continually being placed in a different context and thus generate new insights in debates, publications and exhibitions, among other things; they are of immeasurable significance for the restoration of important buildings and serve as a source of inspiration for new design projects.

The Story of Housing

The Netherlands Architecture Institute has, through this exhibition and book, explicitly chosen to argue for a certain meaning to the collection. By concentrating on housing and on built projects, it argues that one can see the history of Dutch architecture as focused on the realization of the collective domestic environments. Other interpretations and organizations are of course possible, and may be explored by this institution in the future. For now, this survey traces the development of these forms of housing over roughly the last 150 years. It does so mainly with material drawn from the Netherlands Architecture Institute's extensive collections.

This book concentrates on fifteen environments that are most characteristic for their time and the different situations to which architects, builders and clients reacted. In particular, five of these have been elaborated extensively because of the way in which they stand for a number of important developments in Dutch architecture. In the Vondelstraat area of Amsterdam, private developers were given quasi-suburban plots at what was then the edge of the city. Here the importation of foreign styles and urban design attitudes is still prevalent. In Plan Zuid, the rediscovery of a Dutch tradition of housing and its adaptation to the emergence of a large middle and working class were made possible and guided by the negotiated partnerships engendered by the Housing Act. In Pendrecht, the abstraction of such forms, the development of modular 'stamps' and the application of new technologies answered the optimism of the post-Second World War era, promising light and air for everyone. Almere, currently still emerging on land reclaimed after the Second World War, is the largest new town developed after this period. Already partially under renovation, it shows the continual attempts to learn from the cultural legacy of Dutch housing in a completely new and artificial situation. Along the way, it exhibits the latest experiments in the field. A fifth focal point, finally, is the perennially unbuilt neighbourhood of the future. In the utopian visions of architects unfettered by the realities of construction or legal restraints, more radical versions of the Dutch domestic scene are visible.

These fifteen environments are analysed by architectural historians and critics. Together with the illustrations, which form an autonomous body of information within this project, the book and the exhibition at the Netherlands Architecture Institute it accompanies tell the story of housing that makes a collective environment on an unstable land in which each resident can find a distinct place to be at home.

Aaron Betsky (NAI Director) and **Mariet Willinge** (Head of NAI Collection)

1865-1882
Vondelstraat Amsterdam

Vondelstraat

P.J.H. Cuypers used the proximity of the Vondelpark to shape his romantic vision of urban living. This picturesque cityscape of houses in greenery around a church, in its almost village-like intimacy, mimics the atmosphere of a Catholic parish.

photograph from the commemorative book published on the occasion of Cuypers' 90th birthday, 1917

View from the Vondelpark in the direction of the Vondelstraat, with Cuypers' double residence, Nieuw Leyerhoven (left) and the Heilig Hart church (photo circa 1915)

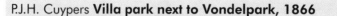

P.J.H. Cuypers **Villa park next to Vondelpark, 1866**

NAI collection, Cuypers archive

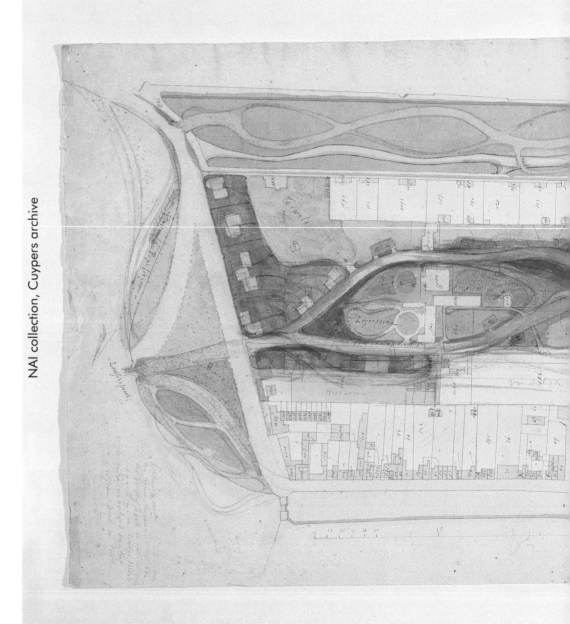

The upscale residential area lay between the Overtoomsche Vaart (later the Overtoom; bottom) and the Vondelpark (top). On the left, the future Stadhouderskade is indicated by dashed lines, with existing buildings in pink. The meandering streets

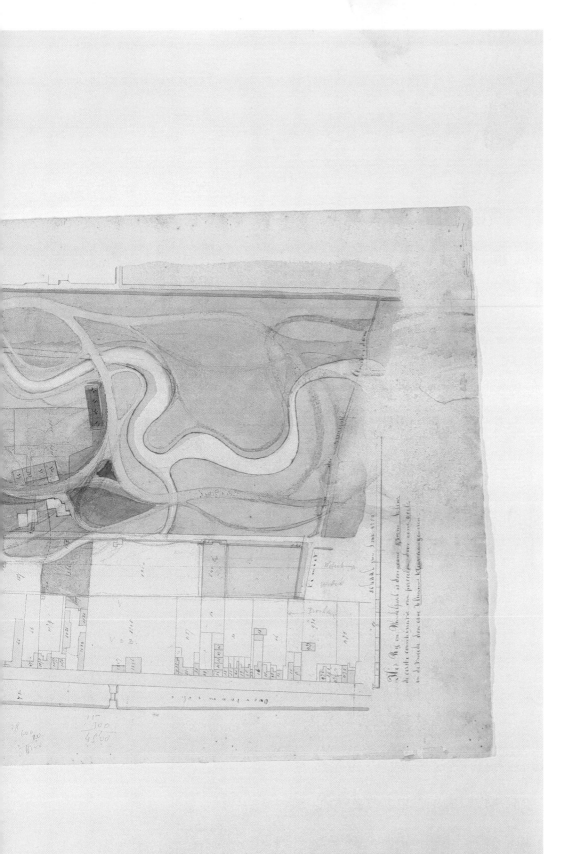

loosely dotted with villas (dark red) are clearly derived from the layout of the Vondelpark. The existing country seat of Oud-Leyerhoven, Cuypers' first Amsterdam residence, lies encircled by streets in the centre of the plan.

P.J.H. Cuypers **Complex of three residences, Vondelstraat 44-48, 1870, façade detail**

NAI collection, Cuypers archive

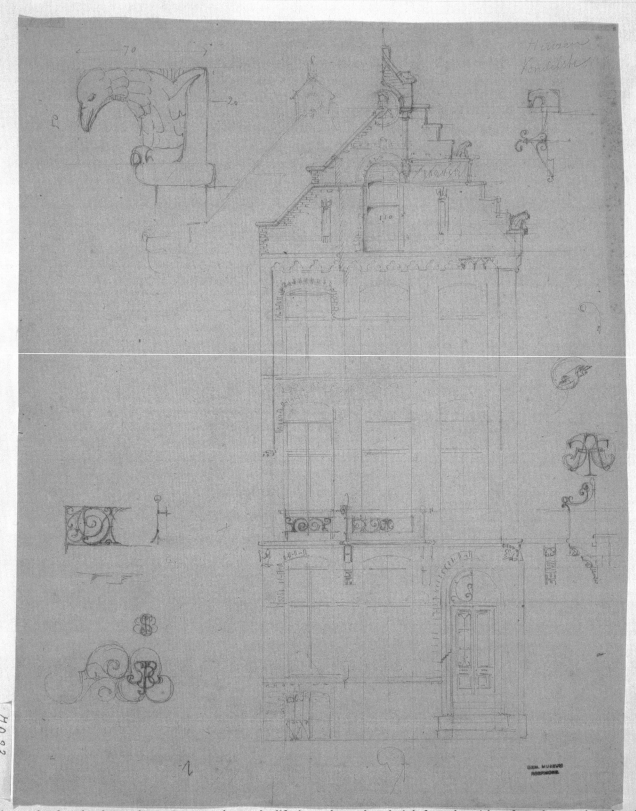

This study clearly shows how Cuypers brought life into the sober brick façade with a few decorative details that do not disrupt, but in fact underscore, the façade's composition. The classical canal façade scheme – narrow, three storeys, with the entrance on the side – was the standard; decorative details could vary.

P.J.H. Cuypers **Double villa including own residence, 1881, sitting room and office in own residence (photo 1897)**

photograph from Architectura magazine, 16 May 1897

The interior as total artwork: woodwork, furniture (including lamps), stained glass and floor coverings were all designed by Cuypers himself. Note the (illegible) text above the sliding doors.

1865-1882 VONDELSTRAAT AMSTERDAM

P.J.H. Cuypers **Heilig Hart van Jezus Catholic church, Vondelstraat, 1871-1880, east side**

This drawing clearly shows how the church is actually seen as one large spire that dominates the entire Vondelstraat and its environs as a powerful urban-planning accent. Its exterior, therefore, was deliberately kept sober. Only the spire itself was more richly detailed. The Vondelpark is indicated to the left; Cuypers would later build Nieuw-Leyerhoven here. The church was converted into offices in the 1980s and is no longer open to the public.

P.J.H. Cuypers **Heilig Hart van Jezus Catholic church, Vondelstraat, 1871-1880, main entrance door hinges**

For the decorative detailing of his buildings, Cuypers had his own studio for industrial and applied arts, the Kunstwerkplaatsen (Workshops) Cuypers en Co in Roermond, whose crafstmen and artists he personally trained.

P.J.H. Cuypers **Double residence Nieuw Leyerhoven, Vondelstraat 73-75, 1876-1877, initial façade design**

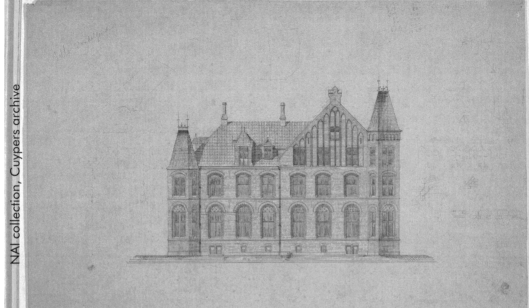

NAI collection, Cuypers archive

This is the first of four façade variants. The asymmetry in the façade disguises the fact that this consists of two houses with identical floorplans. The Gothic tracings in the upper gable are noteworthy. The lattice work in coloured brick above the lower windows is typical of Cuypers.

P.J.H. Cuypers **Double residence Nieuw Leyerhoven, Vondelstraat 73-75, 1876-1877, initial design**

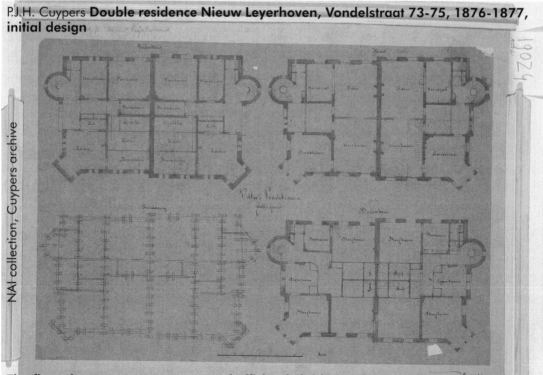

NAI collection, Cuypers archive

The floorplans are very compact and efficiently laid out. The introduction of a spiral staircase in a separate staircase tower especially saves space. One unusual feature is that while there is no separate dining room, there is a music room.

P.J.H. Cuypers **Double residence Nieuw Leyerhoven, Vondelstraat 73-75, 1876-1877, east and rear elevations of Vondelstraat 73 from the Vondelplantsoen (photo circa 1900)**

NAI collection, Cuypers archive

The entrance with raised stoop is located on the right, next to the stairwell. The many extensions and additions create a picturesque effect, although the external architecture remains sober. At far left, the rear façade of Cuypers' own residence, located next door (Vondelstraat 77-79), is visible.

This monumental boarding house demonstrates the mobility of metropolitan life and the resulting demand for temporary housing.

NAI collection, Cuypers archive

Th. J. Cuypers **Oud Leyerhoven** boarding house, corner of the Vondelstraat and the Tesselschadestraat, 1884-1885, façade on the Tesselschadestraat with entrance

A continuous frieze of tile panels demonstrated an attempt to culturally elevate everyday life. The representation of the Muses – personifications of the fine arts, in this case music – on the façade of a lodging house was an unusual and telling gesture.

NAI collection, Cuypers archive

J. Th. J. Cuypers **Oud Leyerhoven** boarding house, corner of the Vondelstraat and the Tesselschadestraat, 1884-1885, Tesselschadestraat façade detail

1865-1882 VONDELSTRAAT AMSTERDAM

A raised cellar elevates the house above the street level. From balconies on the street façade, the residents can literally look down on the passers-by. The effort to achieve representational impact is most obvious in the façade on the Tesselschadestraat, where the windows are combined into a monumental whole.

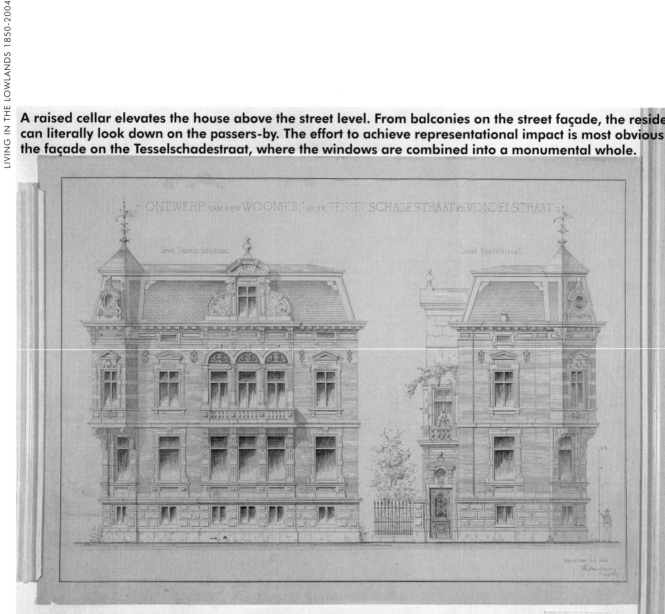

NAI collection, Van Gendt archive

A.L. van Gendt **Witteveen residence, corner of the Vondelstraat and the Tesselschadestraat, Amsterdam, 1880-1882, façades on the Tesselschadestraat (left) and Vondelstraat (right)**

A representationally impressive neo-classicism also dominates inside. The vestibule and staircase form a monumental focal point. In the rear the atmosphere is more informal: here the house opens up to the garden through balconies and a pergola.

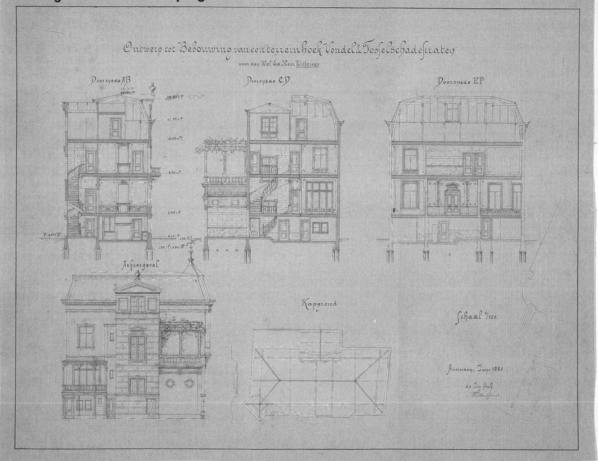

NAI collection, Van Gendt archive

A.L. van Gendt **Witteveen residence, corner of the Vondelstraat and the Tesselschadestraat, Amsterdam, 1880-1882, cross-sections and rear elevation**

P.J.H. Cuypers Bierhuis Vondel for G.A. Heineken, Vondelstraat 43, 1873-1874, side elevation with entrance

NAI collection, Cuypers archive

The whole is designed like a villa, with Cuypers' typical mix of neo-Gothic and chalet styles and even half-timber on the second level. The essentially ordered construction is disrupted by all manner of recesses and projections, balconies and bays, so that a picturesque whole emerges. The beer house was initially surrounded by a beer garden, but was soon absorbed into the structure. Along with several buffets and rooms, there was a skittles alley in the cellar and a billiards hall on the first level. In 1903, the building underwent massive renovation and was turned into a Masonic lodge.

The relatively modest entrance gate topped with a residence on the Vondelstraat led, via a passage, to the stables complex and the large covered riding school. Equestrians would also venture from the riding school into the Vondelpark. In 1889, an extension as far as the Overtoom (the Vondelkade at the time) followed, including two coach-houses and stalls. In 1969 part of the extension was torn down, and the rest was also threatened with demolition, but the whole complex was restored by B. van Kasteel around 1980 and still operates as a riding school.

Oasis in a stone desert
Jean-Paul Baeten

The Vondelstraat in Amsterdam combines three typical nineteenth-century phenomena: urban living in a green setting, private town planning and the Catholic emancipation struggle. In the same period that European cities like Berlin with its Ring and Paris with its boulevards were developing into majestic and modern metropolises, in Amsterdam it seemed impossible to devise an expansion plan that exceeded the scale of just a few streets. In France and Germany, a highly centralized authority could exact the realization of grandiose plans; something which was impossible in the liberal-democratic Netherlands. Amsterdam's liberal city council had confidence in private initiative and left the expansion of the city in the hands of private speculators. The result was inchoate and grim neighbourhoods, to which the Vondelstraat's allure was an agreeable exception.

Thanks to the proximity of the Vondelpark, in the Vondelstraat the ideal of country living could be combined with urban amenities into a luxury living environment of villas and desirable townhouses for a new urban elite. It was unusual that in this instance a renowned architect, P.J.H. Cuypers (1827-1921), performed as project developer, supported by leading figures from the Catholic emancipation movement, such as J.A. Alberdingk Thijm and V. de Stuers.

Though speculative considerations played their part, there was also a cultural-political agenda underlying the whole undertaking. As early as 1867, a statue of the 'people's poet' and Catholic convert, Vondel, was placed in the park on the initiative of Cuypers, Alberdingk Thijm and others, with a socle designed by Cuypers. Street and park were later named after him. A few years later, partly on Cuypers' initiative and to his design, a Catholic church towered skyward in the axis of the extended Vondelstraat. Church and monument were linked by a public garden. This constituted an important point in the Catholic emancipation struggle, all the more because the church was financed from the proceeds of a national lottery, supported by Queen Sophie (wife of king Willem III). The conjunction of neo-Gothic, religion and nationalism was typical for the later 'Gothic Revival', which became highly influential between 1850 and 1914, first in England and later also in the Netherlands, Belgium, France and Germany.

In 1865, Cuypers moved from Roermond to Amsterdam on the advice of his friend, the writer and critic, J.A. Alberdingk Thijm. At this juncture Cuypers was already a leading architect who had primarily made his name as an architect of Catholic churches following the restoration of the Catholic episcopal hierarchy in 1853. For Cuypers, being based in Amsterdam meant the possibility of a definitive breakthrough to the national stage. Two years earlier he had won the second prize in the competition for the Museum Koning Willem I, the later Rijksmuseum. This success made him hungry for more. Via Alberdingk Thijm, he quickly came into contact with a Catholic cultural elite of writers, artists and musicians, but also with politicians, lawyers and bankers. Here lie the origins of a Catholic network in Amsterdam, which within 20 years would result in him hauling in prestigious

commissions like the Central Station and the Rijksmuseum.
On the advice of people belonging to these circles, Cuypers immediately bought Oud–Leyerhoven. This old inn with a large tea garden just outside the former Leidsepoort city gate, between the Overtoom – then still a raggedly built-up country lane alongside a busy waterway – and the Nieuwe Park (known as the Vondelpark from 1867), which was still under construction. He converted the complex into a house and studio. Cuypers was speculating on future developments with this purchase. The park, designed by the landscape architect J.D. Zocher (1791-1870), was established on the initiative of a committee of leading citizens. They had founded the Vereeniging Rij- en Wandelpark ('Association for the Riding and Walking Park') in 1865 with the objective of establishing a new city park, since urban greenery was scarce in Amsterdam. In perfect keeping with the liberal tradition, improving the look of the city was considered a civic duty. The acquisition of land and construction of the park were defrayed by collection efforts and the sale of surrounding plots of land. 'Urban beautification' and speculation went hand in hand here. Turning a worthless marsh-land area just outside the city into a park meant that the adjoining land could be sold as expensive construction land for villas. Such villa neighbourhoods were typical for the rapidly expanding cities of the second half of the nineteenth century. Many new business-men were economically tied to the city, though they thought it too congested and dirty to live there. A country house was often too far away and overly expensive, so a villa district was a good compromise.

Together with the experienced speculator-architect N. Redeker Bisdom, who had also purchased land here, Cuypers developed a plan for a park-like villa neighbourhood adjacent to the new park. Moreover, when selling plots of land around the park, the Vondelpark Association always stipulated that no working-class housing could be built there. This safeguarded the status of the Vondel quarter and thus the value of land there. The city council backed this policy. A similar stipulation applied for the Vondelstraat as well. Cuypers asked for the cooperation of the city council for the laying of streets; the necessary land would then be donated. That was the normal procedure at the time.

It was during this period that Amsterdam started to experience a renaissance after a long period of economic stagnation. Owing to the Industrial Revolution and the unification of Germany in 1870, international trade was growing and Amsterdam was also plucking the profits. The population increased from 240,000 in 1859 to 360,000 in 1884. Over the same period, rents increased by 50 percent, an indication of the encroaching housing shortage. Large numbers of workers were accommodated in the impover-ished city centre, mainly in the Jordaan. The established elite still lived within the grachtengordel, the concentric semicircle of canals. For ambitious newcomers like Cuypers there was no longer any space within the old city boundaries. The city was literally bursting at the seams. In 1865, the year of Cuypers's arrival, the city's last fortifications and city gates were demolished. The area outside the Singelgracht, then still countryside, quickly became a chaotic patchwork quilt, where old country seats and farmhouses were interspersed with new small-scale industries and the attendant housing for workers. Amsterdam still had no official expansion plan. In accordance with the liberal convictions of the city council, businesspeople could buy land and develop their own plans. For bigger plans, the city was often offered land in order to lay streets and sewers. In exchange the city insisted that the streets connected with the existing road network as smoothly as possible.

Cuypers' plan seemed to have the wind behind it. Problems arose unexpectedly nevertheless. Right at the time he submitted his plan, the city council was discussing a first general expansion plan for Amsterdam, which was a carefully kept secret. It was drafted in 1865 by the city engineer J.G. van Niftrik (1833-1910) on his own initiative, in order to bring an end to the chaotic city expansions. It consisted of a ring of neighbourhoods around the existing city, connected by a beltway. Each neighbourhood had a specific character, in keeping with the adjacent section of the old city. For example, a working-class neighbourhood was planned outside the Jordaan, an old neighbourhood for the common folk. In addition, around the Vondelpark and the later Museumplein and adjoining the well-to-do semicircle of historic canals, luxurious residential areas stood arranged in a regular and geometrical street layout. Van Niftrik's plan required large-scale compulsory purchase of land. This not only lacked a legal basis but also the political will of the liberal city council, which wanted to preserve some latitude for private initiatives. Therefore it was never officially approved, though it did form a kind of unofficial blotting-pad in negotiations between private parties and the city.

Cuypers' plan was the first test-case for the new approach. Because it crossed the planned beltway, it shifted developments into a higher gear. On Van Niftrik's advice, the street was straightened and Cuypers was asked to retain a vacant strip 30 yards in width right through the middle of his villa neighbourhood for the later construction of a beltway (the 1e Constantijn Huygensstraat, which was laid in 1872). The adapted plan was approved on 15 January 1867. Over the following years, the Vondelstraat was built up in rapid tempo. The intention was to realize detached villas on the park side, with continuous construction opposite. As there was still no demand for villas, the park side was also constructed with a continuous terrace of more luxurious townhouses. The houses were intended for a new, well-heeled middle class, rich enough to live next to the Vondelpark, but not yet successful enough to have permeated into the traditional elite, a class which preferred a canalside townhouse with a country seat on the river Vecht.

It proved to be a profitable venture for Cuypers and the other landowners, especially the Vondelpark Association. The cost of land rocketed from five to 25 guilders per square metre in the space of a few years. Cuypers soon submitted a request for permission to extend the Vondelstraat. This was prompted by the plans of a neighbouring parish for a new church, which was designed by Cuypers in the axis of the street. For the extension, the city council stipulated that the construction had to be kept more open on the park side, unlike the first section. In order to build in high densities all the same, he often built semi-detached or rows of three linked villas.

Cuypers designed a few detached villas and a number of terraced houses on the Vondelstraat, all in an honest brick architecture with original, craftsman-produced details, which he designed himself, without resorting to the then popular standard ornamentation in plaster and zinc from the factory catalogue. He usually took the initiative himself and built on his own land. Sometimes buyers already presented themselves prior to construction, sometimes only after completion. In this respect he also functioned as a project developer. He built a double house (Vondelstraat 77-79, 1881) for himself. The other houses were often for relations, friends and acquaintances, such as Alberdingk Thijm and the lawyer J. van der Biesen. The latter was likewise active in the Catholic emancipation effort, and helped Cuypers with land deals and in negotiations with the city council.

Cuypers' ideas about domestic architecture were ideologically tinted. The picturesque cityscape of the medieval city was an important source of inspiration, not just in a formal but also an ideological sense. In this respect, the Vondelstraat and especially the ensemble around the Heilig Hartkerk ('Sacred Heart Church') can be read like a manifesto. The street is handled as a collection of individually designed houses with the church as the dominant and connecting element. Cuypers attempted to reconcile civic liberty and individualism with the collectivist ideals of the Catholic class-based society inspired by the medieval guilds system.

As with all the designs by Cuypers, this ideal was also reflected in his houses by his quest for crafted purity and the integration of applied arts and architecture in the form of a fitting decoration scheme for both interior and exterior. An important source of inspiration was the work of the French architect and theorist E. Viollet-le-Duc (1814-1879), who developed a rationalized neo-Gothic style that was also suitable for bourgeois architecture. With their lively and irregular forms, houses by Cuypers are picturesque and especially homely. They do not provide representative backdrops for receptions, but breathe the informal intimacy of family life. At the same time they demonstrate the ideal of the cultural 'elevation' of daily life. For example, the frequent design of a music room for even the smaller houses is remarkable. In practice this also meant throwing into relief the simplicity of an unadorned brick wall, enlivened by expressive details which gave each house a personal stamp, depending on the resident and location. The neo-Gothic style of Cuypers' churches was less suitable for domestic architecture. The houses in the Vondelstraat show how he experimented with late-Gothic and Dutch Renaissance motifs, in search of a new vernacular for city living. Particularly with the detached houses, the spaces are grouped freely, whereby the exterior enjoys a picturesque randomness. That is further emphasized by the frequent use of bay windows, which symbolize domesticity. Decorative details such as tile tableaux, mosaics, paintwork and sculptural details sometimes reveal information about the resident and his (cultural) interests or they portray generally held values such as homeliness and security.

A fine example is the semi-detached house Nieuw-Leyerhoven (Vondelstraat 73-75, 1876-1877), which stands next to the Vondelkerk and overlooks the garden that connects the church and the Vondel statue. The asymmetrical street elevation is treated as a single entity. Due in part to the entrances being set to the sides, the fact that it is two houses is not evident. The design with plain brick walls is simple, with only a few decorative details. The asymmetrical corner bay windows create a picturesque effect. That picturesque informality is even more marked on the side elevations and to the rear, which are turned towards the park. Here extensions such as the entrance-hall, the round stairwell towers and wooden verandahs and balconies afford it a more relaxed atmosphere, in harmony with living in a green setting. The interiors also evoke an atmosphere of informal domesticity. The rooms are relatively small and close together, connected by a short hallway and a staircase. The programme is still fairly luxurious, with a music room, a sunny conservatory and a wine cellar. The servants probably slept in the attic.

Unfortunately, none of the interior designs of the houses in the Vondelstraat have survived, but a rare interior photo of the house next door to Cuypers' own residence (Vondelstraat 77-79, 1881) shows the house as a jewelry box: simple from the outside but full and lavishly decorated inside. The gothically tinged design of the furniture fits in with the architectural style. Texts on the walls and leaded glass windows provide a commentary on family life. For the terraced houses on the north side of the Vondelstraat, Cuypers turned to the architecture of the sixteenth and seven-teenth-century canalside merchants' houses, which he interpreted in a highly personal manner. The layout also derives from this type, with an entrance and a long corridor to the side with a succession of rooms running off it. The simple brick elevations are enlivened by expressive details. For example, the balcony balustrades of Vondelstraat 44-48 (1870) integrate the monograms of the erstwhile residents, Alberdingk Thijm and Van der Biesen.

There is a striking contrast with some houses realized by the architect A.L. van Gendt (1835-1901) at about the same time, where it is the representative rather than the domestic that takes the foreground. Van Gendt was the prototype of the commercial businessman-architect, building efficiently and functionally using the most modern techniques and adapting to the tastes of his clients as regards design. He maintained good contacts with Amsterdam's new business elite and realized countless private and public buildings for these patrons. One of his most famous buildings is the Concertgebouw (1888). His work exudes the dynamism and cosmopolitan atmosphere of large European cities like Vienna and Paris, which Amsterdam's nouveau riche liked to take as their example. Just like the old elite, the arrivistes preferred a representative neoclassicism, but there is scant evidence of the 'noble simplicity' of an earlier generation of architects such as J.D. Zocher. In its overdone ornamentation and the grandiose vestibule, the Witteveen house in particular (corner of Vondelstraat and Tesselschadestraat, 1880) glaringly betrays a desire to impress that is typical of the regained self-confidence of Amsterdam in this period.

On the corner directly opposite, Cuypers' son Jos – J.T.J. Cuypers (1861-1949) – built the luxury Oud-Leyerhoven boarding house in 1884, his very first design, which displays a more original concep-tion of monumentality. At the same time, as a lodging-house, it demonstrates the mobility of modern city life. Even in the new Vondelstraat, people were continually rebuilding and moving house. Leyerhoven had stood on this spot, the old country inn where Cuypers had first lived, until he moved elsewhere in the Vondelstraat. Because of its function and size, the boarding house cannot be read as a house but as a representative public building, propagating the synthesis of art and life in its decorative get-up. Although Jos Cuypers placed his personal accents, it is mainly the influence of his father's monumental style that is recognizable in the combination of plain brick facades and monumental tile tableaux, as employed by Cuypers senior for the Rijksmuseum, for example.

Besides this boarding house, between 1870 and 1890 the Vondelstraat was enriched with a few public amenities which underpinned the increasingly important function of the Vondelpark as an urban recreation area: the Vondel beer house by Cuypers (1871) and the covered manege designed by Van Gendt (1881). As the second entrance to the Vondelpark, the Vondelstraat became a favourite area for the promenading flâneur, a boulevard on an Amsterdam scale where the game of seeing and being seen could be played in an attractive ambiance. The many balconies on the front elevations of the houses also indicate this. Here one can clearly sense the atmosphere of a new, worldlier Amsterdam, the modern big city into which it started to develop in the 1870s. Amsterdam had definitively outgrown the historic ring of canals, and an official expansion plan was eventually formulated in 1877, even though the scale and allure of Vienna or Paris remained beyond reach.

The Vondel beer house with its halls, skittles alley and terraces was the modern urban version of the roadside inns and country houses which had always stood in this area. The client was the brewer G.A. Heineken, who used the picturesque silhouette in advertising campaigns as a trademark – a sign that Cuypers' aesthetic was also starting to catch on in wider circles. Although very different in design, Van Gendt's manege (1881), which was inspired by the renowned Spanische Reitschule in Vienna, is in keeping with the same atmosphere.

New streets and neighbourhoods sprung up all around the Vondelstraat at this time. With the laying of the Tesselschadestraat (1878, to a design by Cuypers), the Constantijn Huygensstraat and the Stadhouderskade, the Vondelstraat was definitively transformed from being a suburb to being an integral component of the new Amsterdam. In 1911, that rite of passage was given a fitting, musically tinted crowning with the construction of a monumental shop with a music hall for a dealer in pianos and 'phonolas' on the corner of Vondelstraat and Stadhouderskade. The street itself has remained something of an oasis, thanks to the spacious layout and especially the monumental accent of the Vondelkerk. In 1924, a critic called the street the first Amsterdam example of 'modern urban beauty'.

1916-1917
Philipsdorp Eindhoven

Eikenlaan
Eindhoven
Iepenlaan
Lindenlaan
Wingerdlaan

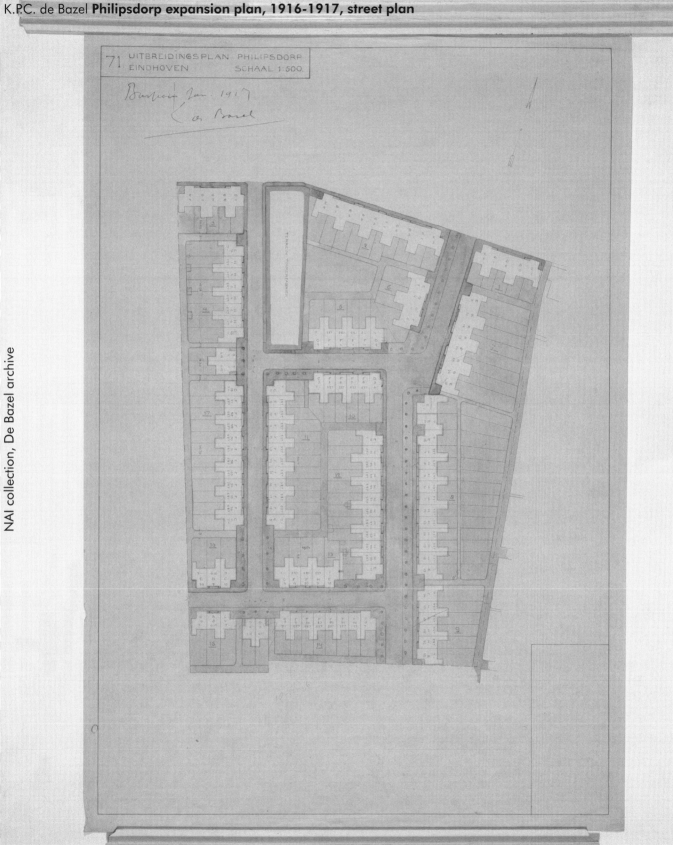

71. UITBREIDINGSPLAN PHILIPSDORP
EINDHOVEN   SCHAAL 1:500.

De Bazel's extension plan shows the composition of streets and building blocks containing 129 dwellings. The open space will not be a lawn, but rather is reserved for the construction of the Philips carpentry plant (1920).

K.P.C. de Bazel **Philipsdorp expansion plan, 1916-1917**

UITBREIDING van PHI
K. de BAZEL

Architect De Bazel presents his plan as a quaint village in a pastoral setting and not as a working-class quarter in an industrial city.

RP TE EINDHOVEN
T B.N.A.

GETEEKEND DOOR
A.C.A.ROTGANS. FEB16.

K.P.C. de Bazel **Philipsdorp expansion plan, 1916-1917, urban plan**

NAI collection, De Bazel archive

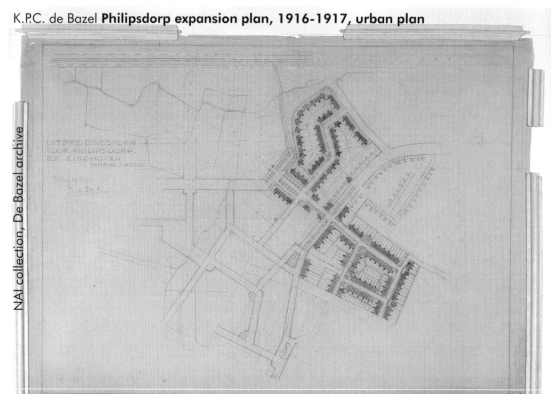

This plan shows the expansion of the Philipsdorp by K.P.C. de Bazel (bottom right) in relation to the first Philipsdorp from 1910 by city architect L. Kooken.

K.P.C. de Bazel **Philipsdorp workers' dwellings, 1916-1917, dwelling floor plan**

NAI collection, De Bazel archive

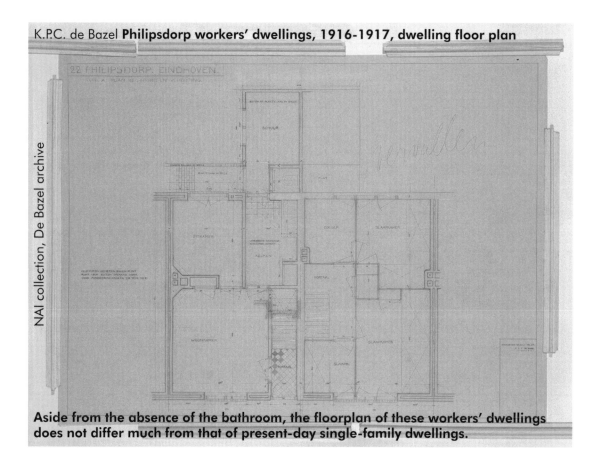

Aside from the absence of the bathroom, the floorplan of these workers' dwellings does not differ much from that of present-day single-family dwellings.

UITBREIDING VAN PHILIPSDORP TE EINDHOVEN • K. DE BAZEL, ARCHITECT.

In the first Philips town, streets were named after members of Anton Philips' family. In De Bazel's extension, the streets were named after trees and shrubs.

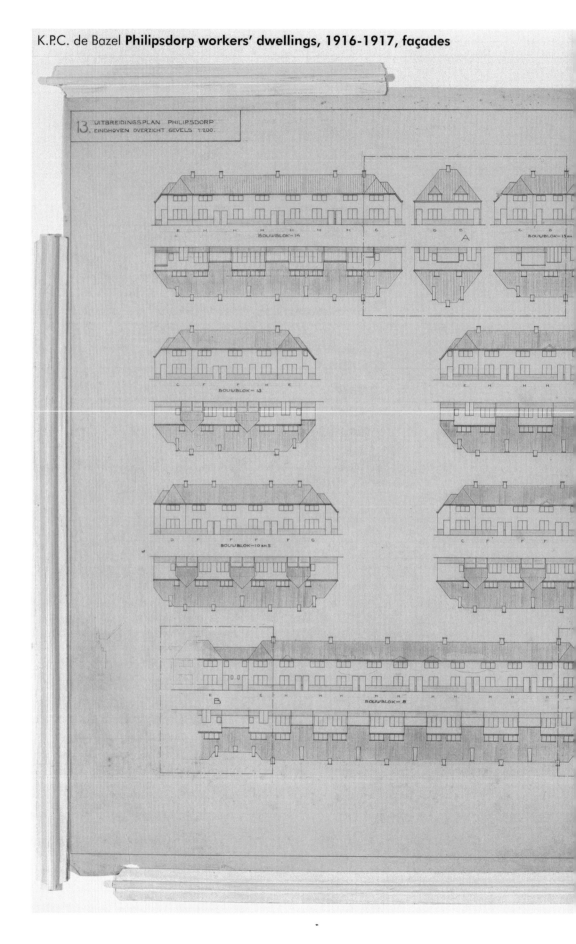

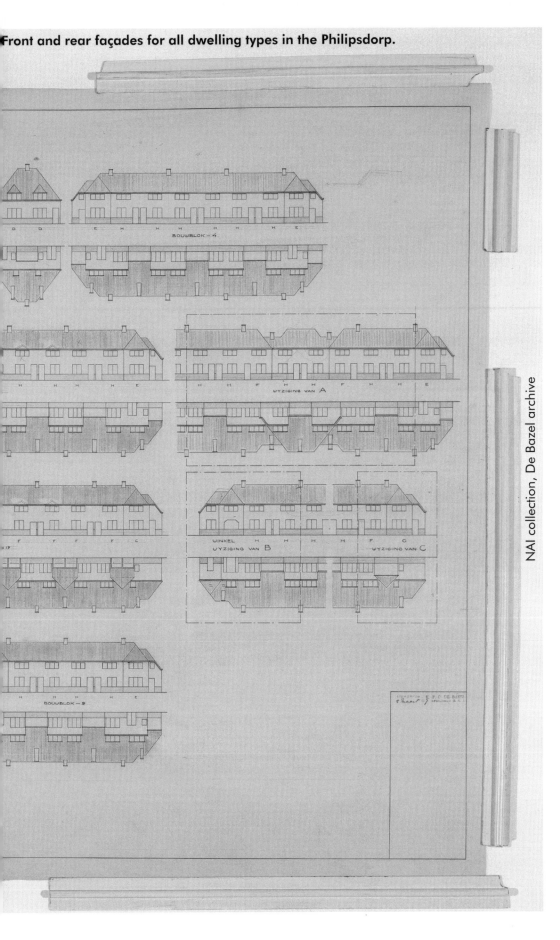

NAI collection, De Bazel archive

K.P.C. de Bazel **Workers' dwellings, Wingerdlaan, 1916-1917 (photo circa 1918)**

NAI collection, De Bazel archive

The completed Wingerdlaantje, with plantings. The street ends at a semi-detached house on the Iepenlaan.

K.P.C. de Bazel **Philipsdorp workers' dwellings, 1916-1917 (photo circa 1918)**

NAi collection, De Bazel archive

The quaint village atmosphere comes to an abrupt halt, and it is clear why these houses are located here: as housing for the workers in the Philips factories.

Eternal boredom, happily
Vladimir Stissi

Walk through Philipsdorp on a drizzly midweek morning in autumn
and you will see what you can see in towns and villages all over the
Netherlands: rows of sound but not exactly exciting houses, streets
with plenty of cars, here and there a tree, and hardly any people.
The facades are well maintained, there are still curtains hanging in
front of the windows, and the streets are neat and tidy. A trim and
tidy predecessor of the VINEX districts, it seems. The only visual
incongruity is the colossal PSV football stadium that looms above
the little houses everywhere: we're in Eindhoven! It is also somewhat surprising how industrial buildings pop up here and there
between the terraced houses.
If you type in 'Philipsdorp' as a search term in a search engine and
the Internet seems to confirm the idyll. A playground association
which seems to be flourishing, at least in virtual terms, accounts
for the first three results, and then there are two references to the
neighbourhood's own former little railway station. Then, however,
we are suddenly dealing with the harsh reality of the twenty-first
century. Hit number six: 'Social characteristics of Philipsdorp.
A study in the context of integral district renewal.' It turns out that
the idyll is obfuscating a potential restructuring of the neighbourhood. To be honest, the study does not elucidate the motives for
renewal. Philipsdorp may well score below average on all social
fronts, but as long as there are sub-districts with detached houses
that score above average, then this is nothing unusual. Moreover,
if Philipsdorp is supposed to be in need of renovation, then three
quarters of Amsterdam can also get packing, and Rotterdam is
surely complete hell on earth. It is therefore no surprise that the
residents, as is more often the case, do not identify with the gloomy
vision of the municipality and housing corporation and have set up
the action group 'Toekomst Philipsdorp' ('Future Philipsdorp'). They
evidently do appreciate the proto-VINEX qualities of their neighbourhood, or they perceive these qualities in other dimensions than
do the policy-makers.
Friend and foe now concur about one thing: Philipsdorp is of great
cultural-historical value. The core was recently listed as a protected
townscape, and the oldest structures have been municipal monuments for many years already. While one party sees this as a
reason for conservation and the other as a challenging spring-
board for renewal, both seem to have overlooked the point that
 the current tension between the VINEX dream and the fear of
being reduced to pauperism springs from the very cultural history
whence it came. Specifically, Philipsdorp too is a product of typical
Dutch domestic culture, which combines well-meant and carefully
considered construction 'for the people' with unending complaint
about the result. There is good reason why the term VINEX has
already been mentioned a couple of times. This little backwater of
Eindhoven offers a fine history lesson for future reference, and the
frayed edges that already catch the eye on a first visit afford
intriguing insights.
The somewhat disorderly street layout and the mixed construction
show that Philipsdorp was not constructed in one fell swoop, as a
neat ensemble. Philips first bought one tract of land and then
another, with other parties also buying and developing land in the
meantime. One section of the Philips land was set aside for the

sports grounds of the PSV (Philips Sports Vereeniging – the Philips Sports Association, now a major-league football club) and some Philips factories were built right next to the houses. In addition, the houses for Philips were developed piecemeal. Philipsdorp has thus unintentionally become slightly more architecturally varied than the average Dutch low-rise development.

That variation is also found in the architecture of the houses built after 1910. Philips took charge of construction itself, and initially made use of Eindhoven's then municipal architect, L. Kooken, assisted by C. Smit of Philips. The architecturally fairly traditional result was clearly not entirely to the company's satisfaction. In early 1916, Anton Philips personally called in the Amsterdam-based architect K.P.C. de Bazel (1869-1923), who had already designed a few houses for the Eindhoven elite. This marked a radical change in course. Instead of streets with rows of more or less identical little houses, De Bazel built terraced housing designed as a unified whole and subdivided into short, closed-off little streets with a few exciting little vistas. Staggered facades and architectural accents in the sightlines give extra shape to the streets and imbue the public space with a confidence-inspiring sense of security that one seldom encounters in new construction.

Within De Bazel's robust town-planning framework (which, more-over, extended beyond the blocks he designed himself), the archi-tecture of his rows of houses is surprising frugal and sometimes even boring. The monumentality in composition and detail of De Bazel's work for cities is completely absent, as is the refinement of his more expensive villas and terraced houses. Still, the extended facades are calm and well-balanced in composition, primarily thanks to the low, broad fenestration – radically modern at that time – in the blank facades: large windows for the living spaces downstairs, small windows for the bedrooms above. Brick and tiles set the visual tone; not the high, narrow windows of the traditional Dutch house.

The originality stops once inside: the floor plans for the houses in Philipsdorp are completely in keeping with the single-family dwelling typology that was already standard then and still is today: living space and kitchen downstairs; three bedrooms upstairs. There was as yet no provision for a bathroom and nowadays housing is usually more spacious, but there has been little change since 1916 at least in the cheaper sections of the VINEX districts.

Although Anton Philips praised De Bazel's houses, De Bazel did not receive any follow-up commissions. His designs were more costly than those of his predecessors, and this was in part the cause of troubles with Philips's builders, who wanted to skimp wherever possible. In order to maintain control of things, from 1917 Philips instructed the supervisor Smit to build simplified derivatives of the work by De Bazel, who did, however, still receive a few commis-sions for larger houses elsewhere in the city for Philips' white-collar staff.

All well and good, as long as their houses are reasonably spacious and have no leaks, and providing there are no groups of young-sters hanging out on the streets, then you won't hear the residents of neighbourhoods like Philipsdorp complaining. Perfection without sparkle, lofty intentions at no great expense, and a bit of mess to tidy up for a change, or as something to look forward to – in this context, an apparently boring urban landscape on your doorstep is already wonderful enough. De Bazel understood this instinctively.

1921-1928
Betondorp Amsterdam

Brink
Brinkstraat
Gaffelstraat
Graanstraat
Harkstraat
Landbouwstraat
Onderlangs
Oogststraat
Ploegstraat
Schovenstraat
Sikkelstraat
Tuinbouwstraat
Veeteeltstraat
Weidestraat
Zaaiersweg
Zuivelplein

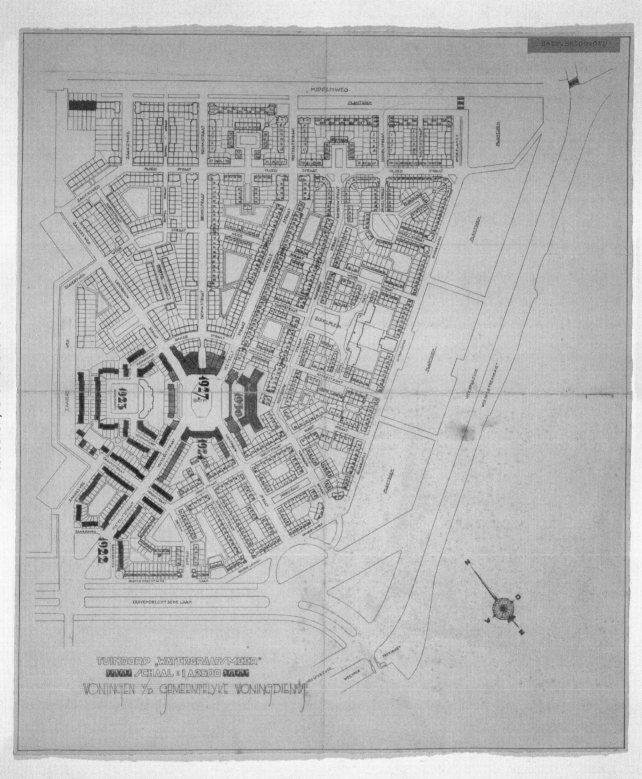

The urban plan for Betondorp developed by J. Gratama and G. Versteeg in 1918 is based on an earlier expansion plan for the municipality of Watergraafsmeer by P. Vorkink and J. Ph. Wormser from 1906-1907.

D. Greiner **Dwellings, Veeteeltstraat, 1923-1924, façade**

NAI collection, Greiner archive

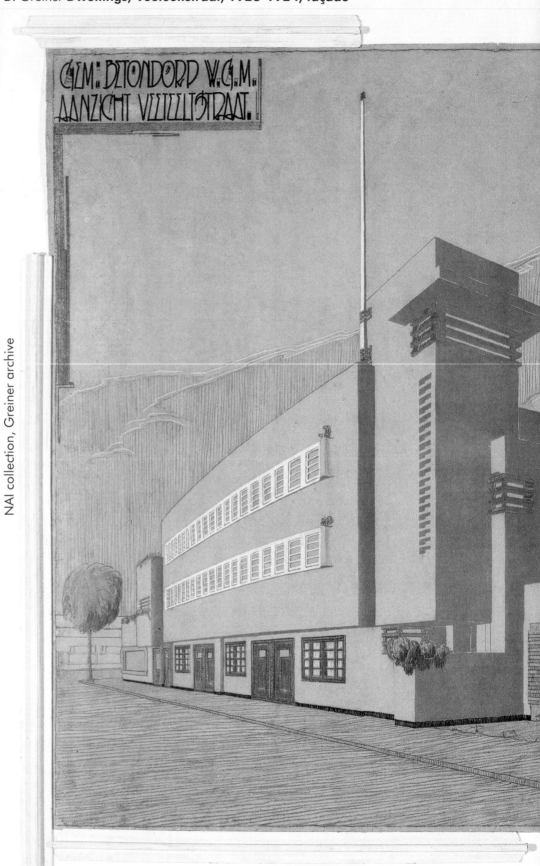

View of the dwellings on the Veeteeltstraat ('Cattle Farming Street'). The rural street names were meant to compensate for the urban aura of the modern construction materials.

D. Greiner **Brink/Veeteeltstraat shops and dwellings, 1923-1924, façade**

To close off the west side of the central square D. Greiner designed a monumental, symmetrical building block with shops. Some of the shops are visible in this presentation drawing. Right, the dwellings on the Veeteeltstraat.

D. Greiner **Shop with dwelling, 1923-1924, floorplans, façades and cross-section**

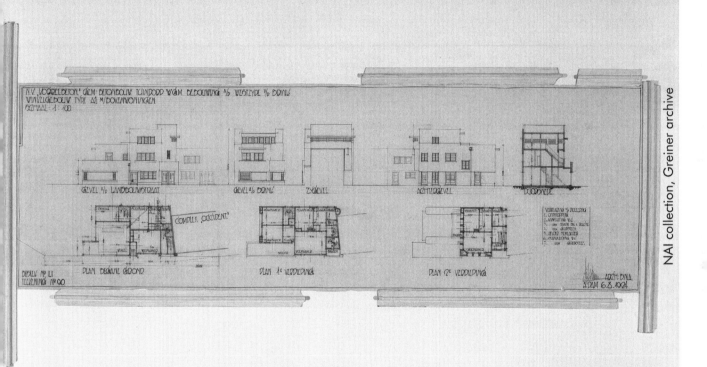

NAI collection, Greiner archive

Corner option for a shop with dwellings on the Brink.

D. Greiner **Public reading room, 1925-1928, façade**

NAI collection, Greiner archive

The public reading room on the Brink, by D. Greiner. The text in the stained-glass windows reads, 'Woe be to him who has read but a single book'. However, as the warning was composed in Latin, only a few will have heeded its edifying words.

D. Greiner **Shop with dwelling at the corner of the Brink and the Landbouwstraat, 1923-1924 (photo 1924)**

NAI collection, Greiner archive

Shop/residential dwelling by Dick Greiner in poured-concrete construction. The shops were situated in prominent locations in 'the village'.

D. Greiner **Dwellings, 1923-1924 (photo 1925)**

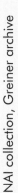

NAI collection, Greiner archive

The dwellings deviated significantly from the traditional Holland brick houses with tiled roofs. So much in fact that the style was dubbed 'Timboectoeaansch' ('Timbuktuesque').

A concrete test plot
Marieke Kuipers

Amsterdam's Betondorp ('Concrete Village') still evokes the atmosphere of an oasis: rustic cosiness with plenty of greenery in the midst of desolate surroundings. When constructed in the 1920s, the immediate surroundings were still a blank canvas, excepting the Nieuwe Oosterbegraafplaats cemetery and the Frankendael country house and estate. Nowadays practically the entire Watergraafsmeerpolder is built up and a raised ringroad funnels through-traffic around the city. The contrast between then and now – between the ground-hugging terraced housing and the towering gallery-access flats on the former Ajax football pitches on the opposite side of the Middenweg – is considerable.

We are now accustomed to houses with flat roofs and facades rendered in plaster and painted in vibrant colours, but at that time the general preference was for traditional houses in brick beneath a tiled roof. Because of the unusual architecture, the concrete houses were sometimes scoffingly characterized as 'something from Timbuktu' – literally associating Betondorp with an exotic oasis. Archetypical Dutch was the norm: one's own little house with a little garden was the domestic ideal for the worker and his family. If there was someone who wished to help realize that ideal then it was A. Keppler (1877-1941), the first director of the Gemeentelijke Woningdienst (Municipal Housing Department) and also brother-in-law to the first Alderman for Housing, F.M. Wibaut (1859-1936). They were both card-carrying, paternalistic socialists. They wanted to emancipate and uplift the worker by means of good housing and education, if necessary with the support of local government. There was good reason for the election slogan of the Sociaal-Democratische Arbeiderspartij (the SDAP, or Social-Democratic Labour Party): 'Wie bouwt? Wibaut!' – 'Who builds? Wibaut!'

As a consequence of the First World War, there was a shortage of housing and high unemployment. Materials were scarce and private building initiatives stagnated. With the Betondorp experiment, Keppler wanted to kill three birds with one stone: break the monopoly of the brick manufacturers, tackle the housing crisis, and ultimately help the unemployed find work. Out-of-work diamond cutters or cigar makers could be employed in the manufacture of concrete blocks with the aid of a cast machine. This job creation and the garden city ideal were deciding factors for the new SDAP alderman, S.R. de Miranda (1875-1942), who took up his post in 1921. The Watergraafsmeer garden suburb was meant to be the showpiece of a constructive and effective social-democrat city government.

Amsterdam eventually achieved the annexation of surrounding municipalities in 1921. Immediately to the east, the neighbouring municipality of Watergraafsmeer had long resisted this move, and in 1906-1907 had independently commissioned P. Vorkink and J.P. Wormser to design an ambitious expansion plan. Anyone who follows the roads which seem to automatically lead to the Brink would hardly suspect that the location of this 'village green' originated in an important junction in that urban plan. This structure was incorporated in the garden city plan devised by J. Gratama (1877-1949) and G. Versteeg in 1918 for the tract of land already acquired by Amsterdam, with a characteristic pattern of radial roadways, connecting streets, cul-de-sacs, squares and public gardens. The hexagonal Brink was eventually completed in 1925-1930 as a veritable crowning, to a design by D. Greiner, and despite its eccentric position it has become the social and urban planning midpoint for the whole area. The bucolic street names were meant to compensate for the urbanity of the modern construction materials, in the same way the nickname 'Betondorp' ('Concrete Village') also hints of a compromise.

While the city council was ensconced in long-drawn-out debate about the costs and amenities for public housing (such as shower and water heater), Keppler made gradual headway towards realizing his 'concrete laboratory' in the future garden suburb. He made a study trip to England, acquired a Winget mould machine, commissioned the construction of various test houses in Tuindorp Oostzaan garden city, and selected seven construction companies for a more extensive test in the Watergraafsmeer polder. It was not until 20 July 1922 that the city council decided to conduct an experiment with 900 concrete houses, in an unequal comparison with the 1,000 brick-built social-sector houses in so-called repetitiebouw (construction with 'repeated design') for the Algemene Woningbouw Vereniging (AWV) and Eigen Haard housing associations. While with the one group the construction materials were controversial, the other group encountered resistance against the extreme standardization of form and layout in housing construction. Fearing monotony and technical shortcomings, the risk was spread over ten different systems for construction in concrete: concrete-block construction (Olbertz/ Bredero, Isotherme, Winget), prefabricated system construction (Bims BetonBouw – also known as BBB, Bron/Occident, Hunkemöller) and monolithic or poured-concrete construction (Korrelbeton, Kossel, Non Plus), as well as the (Dorlonco) steel-frame system. Because of the polder's unstable subsoil, materials had to be lightweight and expensive foundations were to be avoided. Lightweight concrete, which was often mixed with blast-furnace slag and combusted waste, was highly appropriate for this. Within all the strictures in relation to budget, scale, materials and technology, most of the architects succeeded in designing visually attractive and practically organized concrete housing. In principle each system had a different architect. Gratama, for instance, built 200 houses using the Hunkemöller system, which was based on pre-cast concrete elements. These stand on the Tuinbouwstraat, directly opposite its massive association-built housing with portals and steeply pitched roofs. The BBB houses designed by J.B. van Loghem (1881-1940) are dispersed more widely, and were originally immediately recognizable from the geometrical decorations above the paired doors of the upper and lower dwellings. The eye-catching decorations, realized in black varnish, unfortunately disappeared during later renovations.

Greiner worked with two different systems: the advanced Bron system, which made use of facade-wide elements, and non-ferrous Korrelbeton, a concrete made with coarse aggregate. The architect W. Greve from The Hague was involved with the ferrous Korrelbeton variant, having invented a practical form system for this poured-concrete construction method. The houses he designed on the Oogststraat soon gained the nickname 'Misoogststraat' ('Failed Harvest Street'), because the iron remnants in the slag-based concrete started to rust and the walls crumbled. When one of the upstairs dwellings collapsed in 1955, the whole series was demolished and replaced by up-to-date structures.

Luckily, the other Korrelbeton variant has proven more resilient. Greiner used it to realize the important, image-defining neighbourhood amenities around the Brink. Keppler wished to provide accommodation for unmarried workers, a bathhouse and a Montessori school, but these proved too costly. Instead they built shops, middle-class houses, workshops, a clubhouse and a public reading room with library, linked by a concrete pergola. This was followed in 1930 by a series of dwellings for senior citizens in brick. The decorative tower with its clock on the Brink-Veeteeltstraat corner was deliberately designed to form the secular landmark of the garden village. Churches were rejected by the socialists, though a bar was not. There was a café right on that corner. In the midst of the many tee-total prohibitionists it did not survive long, and two churches and a denominational school were added after the Second World War. Both ideology and functions have changed over the course of time. For example, there were about ten storage units for carts for street vendors and shopkeepers on the Landbouwstraat, as well as the office of the municipal estate warden. She came to collect the rent for the council housing every week and en passant kept a beady eye on domestic behaviour. Such control was as characteristic for the then urge to 'improve' people as the domineering placement of the educational centres for young and old. A telling example of this was the leaded glass in the library with the Latin proverb 'Woe be to him who has read but a single book' that urged people to read, inscribed on windows which were also visible to passers-by.

In 1971 the library had to close due to its state of disrepair, and the windows were stolen while it was vacant. Replicas based on the original design drawings were installed during the renovation of 1984. Moreover, five depositories were converted into a community centre for pensioners, so that the library and Brinkhuis again fulfil a central neighbourhood function. The renovation architect for the renovation of the buildings around the Brink was O. Greiner, the son of Dick. The remaining concrete housing was thoroughly renovated by D. Peek in the 1980s.

Remarkably, many local shops have survived. Korrel butchers shop still stands on the corner of the Brink and the Veeteeltstraat. The residents have become deeply attached to Betondorp. The nickname, initially rejected, is now a pet name for the whole garden suburb. Eighty years on, Keppler's 'test plot' still attracts international interest.

1917-1960
Plan Zuid Amsterdam

Beethovenbuurt
Rivierenbuurt
Stadionbuurt

H.P. Berlage **Amsterdam Zuid expansion plan, 1915-1916**

NAi collection, Berlage archive

This map, made for the city council debate in 1917, shows only the planning area that fell within the city limits at the time. Berlage's plan extended south, to the planned south station on a yet-to-be-built ring railway line. The map also shows the complicated situation at the start: polder land with longitudinal parcels and ditches and fragmented ownership arrangements. The contrast between Berlage's plan, which ignores the existing landscape, and the existing built-up area (above in red) with the notorious Pijp district on the right, where the polder ditches dictate the street pattern in order to make construction as affordable as possible, is particularly striking.

H.P. Berlage **Amsterdam Zuid expansion plan, 1915-1916, view from the Amstel onto the east plan area**

NAI collection, Berlage archive

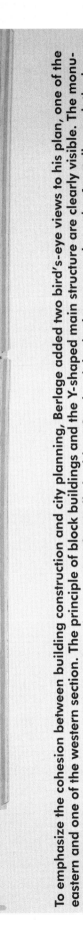

To emphasize the cohesion between building construction and city planning, Berlage added two bird's-eye views to his plan, one of the eastern and one of the western section. The principle of block buildings and the Y-shaped main structure are clearly visible. The monumental block at the bifurcation of the Y later became Staal's Wolkekrabber. On the right, in the centre along the Amstelkanaal, the large hospital complex planned by Berlage can be seen. The P.L. Takstraat-Tellegenstraat housing complex would eventually be built here.

J. Gratama (esthetische supervisie) en anderen **Housing complex with shops for HAGA, Olympiaweg area, 1921-1925, view of the corner of the Olympiaweg (left) and Marathonweg (right)**

Gratama used this perspective to check the effect on the cityscape, namely from the point of view of the passer-by. Corrections in pencil mainly concern the corner construction and the roofline. The added vertical decorations of the hoisting hooks and the roof markings of the portal building are also noteworthy. Note the shops along the Marathonweg.

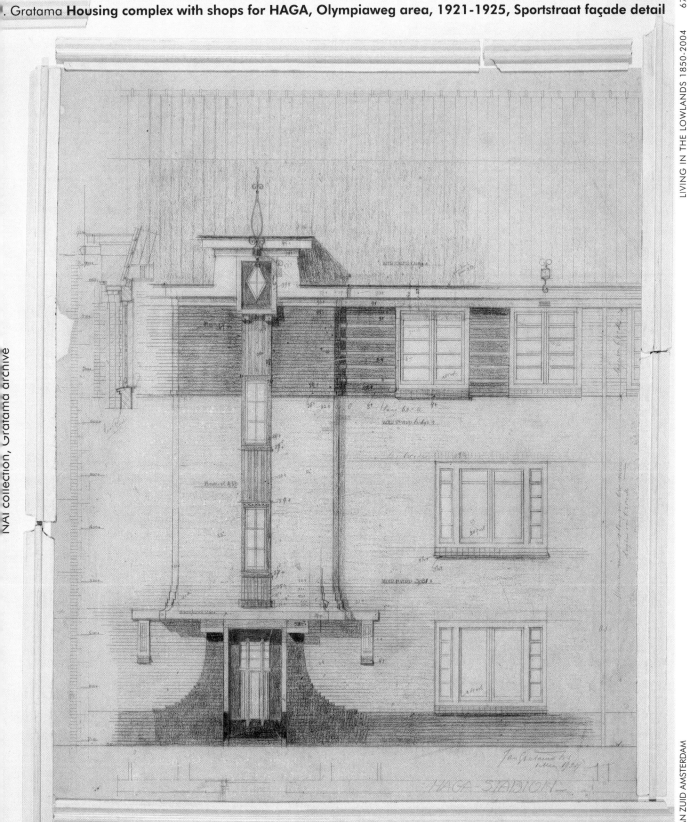

HAGA STADION

Gratama was a master of the use of colour. As throughout Plan Zuid, the base elements are brown brick and red roof tiles. With different colours of brick and strikingly coloured woodwork, he achieves maximum decorative effect with minimum means.

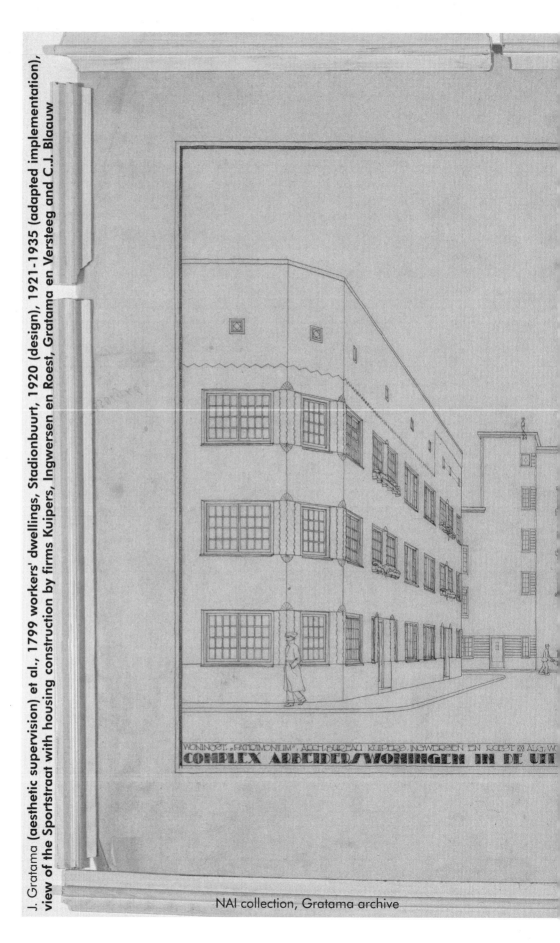

J. Gratama (aesthetic supervision) et al., 1799 workers' dwellings, Stadionbuurt, 1920 (design), 1921-1935 (adapted implementation), view of the Sportstraat with housing construction by firms Kuipers, Ingwersen en Roest, Gratama en Versteeg and C.J. Blaauw

NAI collection, Gratama archive

I.BUREAU GRATAMA EN VERSTEEG IXI WONINGPT. "ONZE WONING" ARCH. C.J. BLAAUW

...1 ZUID BY HET STADION TE AMSTERDAM.

A perspective from a series of eight Gratama had made for the presentation of the overall plan at the Stedelijk Museum in 1921. On each drawing, two or more projects are represented. Along with the identical drawing style, this places the emphasis not on the individual plans but on the urban space they form as a whole.

'Commission of Four' (aesthetic supervision) **ABV housing, Amstellaan area, 1920-1923, façade silhouettes**

NAI collection, Staal-Kropholler archive

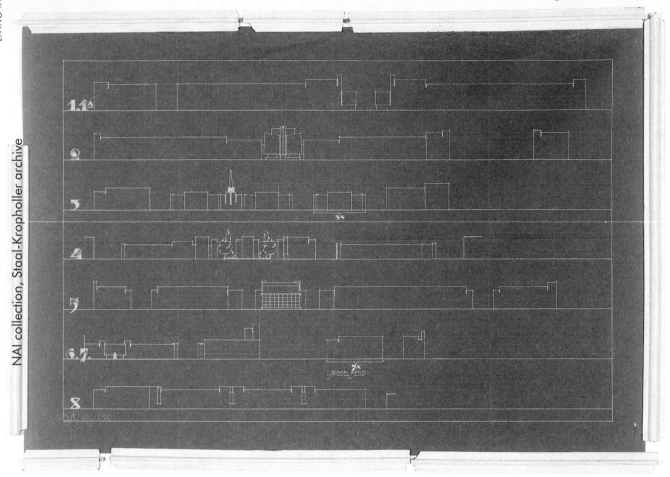

This kind of silhouette drawings served to maintain unity throughout the buildings. Architects were required to limit themselves to filling out the contours indicated. Upper right, the block by De Klerk on the Amstellaan.

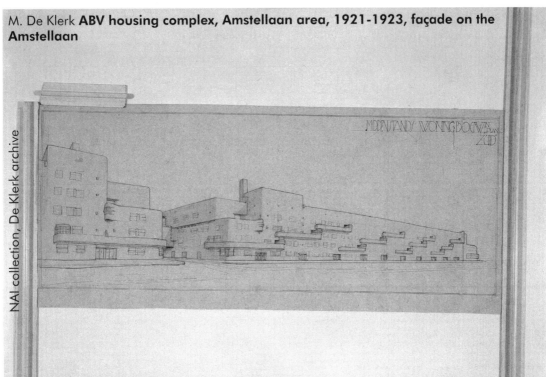

M. De Klerk **ABV housing complex, Amstellaan area, 1921-1923, façade on the Amstellaan**

Here, De Klerk worked for four contractors, each with its own housing programme. His solution to this complex task was brilliant in its simplicity. The sketch shows that De Klerk left out all details and concentrated on the placement and shape of the balconies.

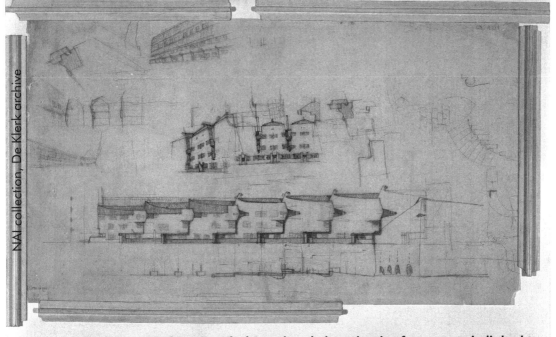

M. de Klerk / P. Kramer **Housing complex for De Dageraad, P.L. Takstraat area, 1918-1923, square façades (top), façade on the P.L. Takstraat (bottom) with variants (above left)**

This sketch demonstrates how De Klerk's uniquely imaginative forms remain linked to the architecture, yet continually test the limits of the possible.

J. Roodenburgh **Closed competition for the Minervaplein, 1926, view from the Minervalaan onto the western half of the square**

NAI collection, Roodenburgh archive

Because of the great interest in the cityscape, a competition was launched for the Minervaplein at the same time as the competition for the Allebéplein. Roodenburgh took part in both. The programme was free, but Roodenburgh opted for closed

PERSPECTIEF

J. GODDENHUISH, ARCHITECT. B.N.A

square façades with monumental shop and office buildings. J. Blaauw's winning plan
would not be completed until after the war.

J. Duiker **Competition Rijksacademie van Beeldende Kunsten, final round, 1917-1918, entrance**

This drawing was made after the competition winner was announced and then shown at many exhibitions in the Netherlands and abroad, including the Exposition des Arts Décoratifs et Industriels in Paris in 1925. The influence of De Stijl is detectable in the angular design. The oblique angle of projection gives the whole a modern, dynamic aspect.

NAI collection, 1923 Jubilee Exhibition archive

**Instead of the Rijksacademie, a public building was stipulated as the centrepiece of the Minervalaan.
Wijdeveld's plan stood out because of its sleekly modern design and the strikingly tall tower blocks, which
the jury felt would cast too much shadow on their surroundings. The building above left stands where the
Rijksacademie was originally planned. J. Boterenbrood's winning plan was never implemented.**

J.F. Staal **Housing complex with high-rise, Daniël Willinkplein area, 1930-1932, west-facing view of high-rise and Zuider Amstellaan (photo circa 1934)**

NAI collection, Wattjes archive / photograph by Van Agtmaal Baarn

View of the skyscraper and the Zuider Amstellaan around 1934. The huge scale of what was then still a virtually empty boulevard, which was meant to connect to a ring road that would not be built until after the war, is striking.

M. de Klerk / P. Kramer **Housing complex for De Dageraad, P.L. Takstraat area, 1918-1923, view of the P.L. Takstraat in the direction of the as yet unfinished Burgemeester Tellegenstraat (photo prior to 1928)**

NAI collection, Wattjes archive

A comparison with De Klerk's sketches shows that the basic idea of the undulating façade has been retained, although its implementation is simplified. Only the towering corner construction in the distance is by Kramer.

J. Gratama **Housing complex with shops for HAGA, Olympiaweg area, 1921-1925, view of the Olympiaweg (photo circa 1925)**

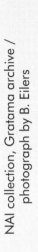

The façade on the wide Olympiaweg was conceived on a large scale, its monumental focal point the portal building with its passage to the quiet inner streets.

J. Gratama **Housing complex for HAGA, Olympiaweg area, 1921-1925, view of the Sportstraat from the underpass on the Turnerstraat (photo circa 1925)**

The contrast between the monumental outer shell and the quiet, almost homely atmosphere of the inner streets within the block is striking. Yet the strict symmetry keeps the streetscape monumental.

Social housing as 'community art'
Jean-Paul Baeten

In 1900, H.P. Berlage (1856-1934), architect of Amsterdam's Beurs, the former Exchange, was awarded the commission to design a southern extension for Amsterdam. The City had purchased 1,380 hectares of land here in 1896. For the first time, the brief specified an aesthetically reasoned plan as the worthy successor to the splendid grachtengordel, Amsterdam's semicircle of concentric canals dug in the 17th century. The first general expansion plan by J. Kalff, dating from 1877, was still in force, but was sooner a practical collage of existing plans without aesthetic pretensions. The Pijp, which was then under construction, was cause for a great deal of criticism of the city council's lack of town planning vision. The government's active role also marked the definitive end of nineteenth century urban planning by speculators, which had produced shabby working-class neighbourhoods like the Pijp.
The selection of Berlage signalled a change of course. At that time, Berlage was one of the most important Dutch architects and one of the few who busied himself with town planning issues. Though this was his first commission for a large-scale urban plan, he had been seeking to devise a modern interpretation of town planning since the 1880s. Through his activities in Amsterdam, he knew that the demands of modern traffic were irreconcilable with the rhythm and scale of the historic ring of canals. He took the monumentality of Haussmann's Paris, 'the most beautiful modern city in the world', with its large-scale, thoughtfully designed construction along boulevards and around squares as his reference point, rather than the picturesqueness of Amsterdam's canals. The problem was that housing predominated in Amsterdam's expansion areas. Unlike in Paris, a monumental vision of the city had to be realized primarily with public housing, without a proliferation of large, civic buildings. This demanded a radical reorganization of housing construction. Though the initial plan, dating from 1900, was unprecedentedly generous in its composition, it still represented a hesitant compromise between romanticism and monumentality. The irregular succession of streets and squares, derived from medieval examples, was inspired by the German theoretician C. Sitte (1843-1903). The large expanses of greenery made the plan prohibitively expensive. Although it was approved by the city council in 1905, it was never realized.
This period saw a number of developmental moves, bringing Berlage's desired monumental vision of the city within reach. Firstly there was the introduction of the Woningwet (Housing Act) in 1901, which obliged the city authorities to oversee the aesthetic and civil engineering aspects of housing construction and to draft an expansion plan. In combination with the founding of government-subsidized housing associations, this at last made it possible to get a grip on mass housing construction.
Berlage also kept himself well-informed about developments in Germany, which was the leading light in the field of modern urban planning. At that time Berlin was already practically demonstrating how mass housing development could be translated into a modern and monumental vision of the city. The key was the combination of large quantities of housing for the working class in large-scale blocks, which in turn constituted the building-blocks for streets, squares and boulevards.

Traffic was another important new element. A voyage to New York and Chicago in 1911 served to further convince Berlage of the fundamental importance of traffic for the modern metropolis. The Housing Act legislated that if a plan was not realized after ten years, then a new plan had to be drawn up. In the second, definitive plan (1915-1917), Berlage took the massiveness of public housing and the scale of modern traffic as his starting point. It was the first practical demonstration of the new urban dimension attributed to public housing by the introduction of the Housing Act. Supported by socialist administrators such as the Alderman for Housing, F.M. Wibaut, and the Director of the Municipal Housing Department, A. Keppler, his goal was to realize 75 percent social-sector housing in the new district. He organized the large blocks of housing into a monumental Gesamtkunstwerk – a total artwork – of streets and squares, completely in line with the late nineteenth-century ideals of the Gemeinschaftskunst – community art – through its aesthetic pretense of having to pursue the betterment and emancipation of the common folk, to 'uplift' them to a bourgeois democratic culture.

The romanticism of the first plan had been replaced by a metro-politan allure, expressed most emphatically by the mainstay of the plan, a symmetrical system of broad boulevards for motorized traffic. The plan was divided into eastern and western sections, separated by the Boerenwetering waterway. Access to the eastern section was via a bridge across the Amstel. From there a large boulevard ran in a westerly direction, the Amstellaan (the later Vrijheidslaan), which branched off into the later Noorder- en Zuideramstellaan (later renamed as the Churchilllaan and Rooseveltlaan) at the Victorieplein. A large hospital complex was planned on the boundary of the Pijp and the new plan. The western section was dominated by the north-south axis of the Minervalaan, for Berlage the ideological and town-planning core of the entire plan. On the south side this monumental residential and shopping boulevard terminated at the station for a new ring railway – for Berlage the ultimate symbol of a new and dynamic mass culture. The new Rijksacademie (State Academy of Art) was planned at the other end, the place where that new mass culture had to be actually designed, completely in keeping with the ideol-ogy of Gemeinschaftskunst – community art. The monumental Minervaplein was set at the midpoint of the Minervalaan. From here there was an east-west boulevard, the later Stadionweg. This connected an artists' house set at the most beautiful point overlooking a confluence of canals in the middle of the plan with a large 'stadium of the people', the later Olympic Stadium, on the eastern perimeter. Here again, art and mass culture were symboli-cally linked.

A second important element was the digging of a new canal, the Amstelkanaal, which ran east-west and split halfway into northern and southern channels at the Boerenwetering. The boulevards and canals were flanked by tall, elongated blocks with housing and shops, alternating with grand squares defined by monumental structures at important junctions. The residential neighbourhoods to the rear had a smaller-scale system of residential streets and squares, often in the form of courtyards. It was schools rather than churches that provided for monumental accents here, in an appropriate translation of the socialist mission to 'uplift' the common folk. Berlage moulded plan and construction into an indivisible whole. He further underscored the significance of that cohesion with a succession of bird's-eye views. These were not first and foremost a question of style, but were based on the street alignments and 'envelopes', the three-dimensional containment of the blocks.

In the execution of the plan, the city council worked together with numerous housing associations as well as with private building contractors large and small. In order to achieve the desired cohesion of the cityscape with this diversity of contractors, a completely new system of aesthetic supervision was devised in conjunction with Amsterdam's architects' associations. Until then, there had only been the schoonheidscommissie – an 'aesthetics commission' – which could assess plans on city land at the request of the city executive of mayor and aldermen. From 1920 there were experiments with a much more far-reaching and more active super-vision of special commissions, which were not solely concerned with the actual plans but also with the cohesion and the connecting fabric of public space. In 1925, a special Commissie Zuid ('Commission for South') of high-level civil servants was set up. Another important instrument was the Dienst Publieke Werken (Department of Public Works), which promoted unity through a uniform design of street furniture, public gardens and bridges. The bridges specially designed by P. Kramer (1881-1961) were important connecting elements, technically and visually, between public space and construction.

Although style, understood as design, was relative for Berlage, cohesion was also the desired objective in this respect. The ultimate measure for the design was the modern, expressionistic work of the Amsterdam School. With its flowing brick facades and richly deco-rative details it was able to conjoin urban plan and construction into a Gesamtkunstwerk pregnant with meaning, and thus illustrate the cultural ideal of Gemeinschaftskunst for all the residents. This new visual vernacular was developed by the architect M. de Klerk (1884-1923) from 1910 on in the context of the increase in public housing, and proved to be ideally suited for grouping dwellings into blocks and blocks into continuous street frontages. His follow-ing was so great that an 'Amsterdam School' was first mentioned as early as 1916. It was this vernacular which became the 'house style' of the new district. Formal idioms which deviated from this, such as the functionalist Nieuwe Bouwen, did not have a chance, and were at best banished to out-of-the-way locations.

Even though Berlage had provided for public housing as the dominant element, the market seemed to follow its own rules. The emphasis in the sections realized first, adjacent to the old city, as well as in the whole eastern section adjacent to the Pijp, was working-class and middle-class housing. In the southwestern section, adjacent to the Vondelpark and Concertgebouw neigh-bourhoods, more luxurious apartments and villas dominated. This was also linked to the economic crisis in the period 1917-1923, when the government tried to stimulate housing construction with generous subsidies. At that time, housing associations played a dominant role, though private enterprises also profited from the subsidies. When the housing construction subsidies were with-drawn, private builders in the western section increasingly shifted their focus to more profitable luxury housing.

From 1917, housing associations realized a number of landmark public housing complexes. In an exemplary cooperation with the socialist city council, the 'workers' palaces' of 'Red Amsterdam' were realized, the pride of their residents as well as cause for international attention. The associations often provided the urban sectoral plans as well, which were always composed of streets, squares and residential courtyards in the spirit of Berlage.

The 'paternalism' went so far as to address even interiors. For example, the 'Samenwerking' ('Co-operation') housing association and a number of other housing associations took the initiative to stage an exhibition about the interiors of working- and middle-class homes in the Stedelijk Museum in 1921. Keppler was responsible for its organization. Alderman Wibaut was also involved with this 'task of cultivation'. A committee of leading architects and furniture designers (including P. Kramer) stipulated requirements for the layout and furnishing of a number of model rooms. The furniture had to be affordable for the working class.

A number of leading designers designed model interiors in a highly simplified Amsterdam School style. Electrical appliances and gas fittings were displayed as well. The exhibition drew a large public and was a great success. They even founded a Centrale Coöperatie voor Woninginrichting ('Central Cooperative for Home Interiors'), which sold cheap, sensible furniture and designed model homes. However, the respected critic J.P. Mieras complained about the condescending paternalism, and it was that same paternalism which resulted in all the new association housing having small, high-set windows overlooking the street, so that the workers could not hang out of the window and gossip.

One of the earliest and most widely discussed examples of association housing is the complex of 294 houses for the housing association 'De Dageraad' ('The Daybreak'), which M. de Klerk and P. Kramer designed in 1920. It was part of a plan for 1,600 units realized by six housing associations on the site where Berlage had planned a hospital. The distinctive design underscores the monumental urban look and simultaneously gives it a wholly novel, picturesque dimension.

A year later, work began on a plan for 1,700 working-class dwellings in the northwestern section, to be designed by eight architects commissioned by nine housing associations and the city council. On Keppler's initiative, this was the platform for the first experiments with a far-reaching form of aesthetic control. Architect J. Gratama (1877-1947), a former colleague of Berlage and also already involved with the urban sectoral plan, had to oversee the overall architectural impression. His brief extended from the silhouette of the elevations overlooking streets and squares to the choice of colour for the window-frames and the street profiles. He designed a complex of 540 units himself, arranged in a number of giant perimeter blocks with internal streets that were accessed via passageways.

The interior layout in plans of this kind was more or less fixed. The same standard floor plans were applied in public housing throughout Zuid, guided by government codes and economic necessity. The role of the architect as orchestrator, moulding a dramatically convincing overall impression from many small sections, is especially clear in the sketches by Gratama. This almost filmic design approach is evoked in the series of perspectives was used to present the whole plan in the Stedelijk Museum in 1921.

A subsequent experiment, in 1922, entailed the construction of 2,000 units on an area of 10 hectares at one of the plan's most prestigious locations, between the Amstel, the Amstelkanaal and the Amstellaan. Seventy commercial builders, joined together in the Amstels Bouwvereniging (ABV, or the 'Amstel Construction Association'), concluded a contract with the city council. The contract entailed the construction of 2,000 units with an average floor area of 100 square metres, which was higher than the norm at the time. The subsidy was 25 guilders per square metre. Types and dimensions were predetermined; only the arrangement of the rooms could vary to any extent. The buildings along the main streets could be four storeys high, the others three.

In consultation with the ABV, the city appointed a 'Commission of Four' for the urban plan and aesthetic supervision, made up of the city architect, A. Hulshoff, and the architects J.F. Staal (1879-1940), J. Gratama and J. de Meijer. The commission drafted the silhouettes of all the street elevations, precisely indicating the outline of projected construction. On this basis, the committee decided which sections were to be placed in the hands of one particular designer. These blocks were then distributed among the builders by drawing straws. An architect was allowed to work with a maximum of four building contractors. The architect first had to draw up an overall design and, on its being approved by the commission, a detailed facade design. The drawings by the architect M. Staal-Kropholler (1891-1966) for the elevation on the Holendrechtstraat precisely illustrate this process. They clearly reveal the pros and cons of the system. Although she worked for four building contractors, the street frontage forms a unified whole. However, the design extends no further than the facade. This led to a great deal of criticism.

At the presentation of the results in the Stedelijk Museum in 1923, even commission member Staal spoke of 'masquerade architecture'. That same reproach included De Klerk, who designed the distinctive block on the Amstellaan. Through his design of the balconies he managed to enliven the whole facade. However, the windows did not connect to the spaces behind and the balconies were inaccessible, so adaptations were called for right away. Nevertheless, on completion, this plan proved to be a success. A convincing new city borough started to grow from the combination of Berlage's urban planning principles and the formal vernacular of the Amsterdam School.

Progress was slower with the monumental accents that Berlage had projected. The station and the Rijksacademie set at opposite ends of the Minervalaan remained unrealized, so the whole plan was in fact ideologically decapitated. The ring railway was only realized much later and construction of the spectacular winning competition design for a new Rijksacademie by Bijvoet and Duiker ground to a standstill on nothing more than its foundations in 1923 due to an economic crisis. Even the August Allebeplein, a later plan, was never realized. Nevertheless, the lane together with the adjoining Apollolaan and the Beethovenstraat became the midpoint of a luxury residential area with villas and apartment complexes. Thanks to the hosting of the 1928 Olympic Games it was possible to realize the stadium that was conceived for the westernmost edge. The stadium forecourt and the monumental tower were defining elements in the stadium neighbourhood, and another of the plan's highpoints, the Victorieplein, was also given an apt accent. The handsome 1931 skyscraper by J.F. Staal, the Netherlands' first residential high-rise, is the true jewel in Plan Zuid's crown. With its design and location, it visually embodies

Berlage's endeavours to monumentalize collective urban living and simultaneously adds a new dimension. The breakthrough from an inward-looking vision of the city to a new metropolitan scale that became palpable here pointed ahead to the first general extension plan for Amsterdam (1929-1932, ratified in 1935), which the architect and town planner Cornelis van Eesteren (1897-1988) was already working on. The starting-point for this plan was no longer a monumental vision of the city like Berlage's, but a rational and functional analysis of the future needs of the city in accordance with the principles of modern urban planning as set out by the Congrès Internationaux d'Architecture Moderne (CIAM). The genius designer made way for an urban planning agency, in which research and the drawing up of plans were combined. Architecture and urban planning were radically divorced. This analytical urban planning would conquer the world after the war.

At the first international CIAM congress on modern urban planning in 1927, Berlage could still justifiably assert that nowhere in the world was the harmony between architecture, urban plan and government so perfectly orchestrated as in Amsterdam. Plan Zuid, which was practically finished in 1940, became the swansong of the classic, aesthetically focused art of urban planning, based on the vision of a genius designer. It is this tradition which has once again been a focus of interest in recent decades, after post-war districts like the Bijlmer had demonstrated the bankruptcy of modernist urbanism. The harmonization of all the details into a great unified whole has ensured that Zuid is still a pleasant living environment, and to this very day it inspires architects and urban planners all over the world.

1915-1954
Hilversum

Adelaarstraat
A. Fokkerweg
Begoniastraat
Bosdrift
Buizerdstraat
Cameliastraat
C. Oolenstraat
Daltonstraat
Diependaalselaan
Dortsmanstraat
Duivenstraat
Edisonstraat
Eksterstraat
Fuchsiastraat
Galvanistraat
Geraniumstraat
H. Aalbrechtstraat
Hilvertsweg
Huygensstraat
J. v.d. Heydenstraat
J. v. Campenlaan
Jupiterstraat
K. Onnesweg
Kievitstraat
Korenbloemstraat
Lavendelstraat
Leemkuilen

Leeuwerikstraat
Leliestraat
L. de Keylaan
Lorentzweg
Marconistraat
Merelstraat
Mezenstraat
Minckelerstraat
Mussenstraat
Nachtegaalstraat
Neuweg
Ooievaarstraat
Planetenstraat
Reigerstraat
Röntgenstraat
Saturnusstraat
Slachthuisplein
Spechtstraat
Sperwerstraat
Spreeuwenstraat
Stalpaertstraat
Valkstraat
Van 't Hoffplein
v.d. S. Bakhuizenstraat
v. Musschenbroekstraa
Vennecoolstraat
Vingboonsstraat
Weberstraat
Zwaluwplein
Zwaluwstraat

General map of the municipal housing complex which at the time was located on the edge of Hilversum's built-up area.

W.M. Dudok **Municipal housing complexes, 1916-1956, general view phasing, 1922**

As city architect, W.M. Dudok called for the institution of a municipal housing authority that, by building and managing housing for the working class, would stimulate people to move out of their inferior dwellings voluntarily.

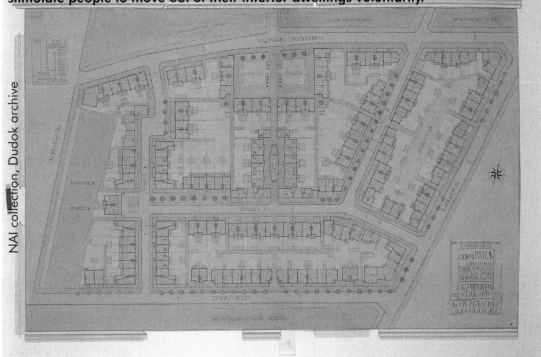

W.M. Dudok **First municipal housing complex, 1916-1918, urban plan**

NAI collection, Dudok archive

In 1916, W.M. Dudok wrote to the Hilversum city council about his plan: 'I have not shied away from a great deal of drawing work, in order to achieve great diversity in dwelling types as well as in appearance and form.'

W.M. Dudok **Eighth municipal housing complex, 1923-1925, façades on the Slachthuisplein**

NAI collection, Dudok archive

The eighth municipal housing complex is situated around the existing slaughterhouse. The green grass field can serve as a cattle market. Cutbacks on construction costs left W.M. Dudok little architectural freedom, resulting in relatively sober buildings around the square.

W.M. Dudok **Gate house, first municipal housing complex, 1916-1918**

NAI collection, Dudok archive / copyright Gemeente Hilversum

According to W.M. Dudok, the central section was progressive in that it incorporated a dwelling above the portal. This construction made it a fitting architectural environment for the modern church.

W.M. Dudok **Dwellings, first municipal housing complex, 1916-1918**

NAI collection, Dudok archive / copyright Gemeente Hilversum

'The correct alternation of the (...) brick walls with white or yellow stucco façades will heighten the picturesque effect, to which the plantings will contribute as well,' wrote W.M. Dudok.

W.M. Dudok **Dwellings with shops, fifth municipal housing complex, 1920-1922 (photo circa 1923)**

NAI collection, Dudok archive / photograph by C.A. Deul

At a prominent spot, the intersection of the Neuweg and Hilvertsweg traffic arteries, two shops were designed.

W.M. Dudok **Dwellings, second municipal housing complex, 1918-1920 (photo 1921)**

NAI collection, Dudok archive

The city council of Hilversum objected to the high rent prices in the second complex. W.M. Dudok defended these by writing that he had fulfilled the various needs of the residents by designing the dwellings in diverse types and rent prices.

W.M. Dudok **First municipal housing complex, 1916-1918**

NAI collection, Dudok archive

Corner of the Anemonestraat and Papaverstraat in the first municipal housing complex.

Dudok and the image of Hilversum
Herman van Bergeijk

The impression that Hilversum leaves etched in the mind's eye of
a visitor is an admixture of chaos and calm. Chaotic is the way the
traffic wriggles its way through the city; calm are the many
neighbourhoods hidden away from the bigger through roads like
secluded enclaves. The architect and town planner W.M. Dudok
(1884-1974) tried to strike a balance between these two extremes.
In part that has succeeded, certainly in the suburbs where he was
given free rein to work as all-powerful architect. In the centre there
is hardly any of his work to be seen. Dudok's road to architecture
was a roundabout one. He initially chose to follow a military career,
where he was confronted with the broad field of the army.
However, his interest was at the same time drawn to designing.
Among other things he designed a barracks which was drafted like
a small town. Even after leaving the army he continued to be a man
fond of strict discipline, so he was no stranger to a certain Prussian
mentality. In addition, he had an eye for absolutely every gradation
of scale, grasping that even the smallest detail could be important.
Thanks indeed to his training, he had become convinced that as an
architect he should not lose sight of the small or the large. Defining
for his conceptualization were the strategic position of towns and
cities, their hierarchical composition from distinct units which
nevertheless had to gel, and the connecting roads to the city and
passing through it.
While at his civilian post in Leiden he broadened the foundations
of his thinking: he created a few important buildings as orientation
points in the cityscape. He was simultaneously working on the city
expansion plan. When he transferred to Hilversum a few years
later, in 1915, he was charged with a great many responsibilities.
As Director of Public Works, besides designing the physical form of
the town, he was also responsible for the tram service, telephone,
electricity, gas and water utilities, cleaning, sewers and the fire
brigade.
The various municipal housing projects in Hilversum show that he
regarded the town as consisting of different 'rooms'. Visual key
points not only had to reinforce the orientation towards the neighbourhood, but also that within it. A school was therefore soon fitted
with a tower, and from afar could be taken for a church. Staggered
building lines, bends in streets and an articulated design of the
built block helped to give the neighbourhood a distinct recogniza-
bility. Dudok also paid careful attention to the form of roofs – the
hat on the head. Public greenery, low walls and flowerpots were
standard elements in designing the neighbourhood. Traffic was
channelled past the neighbourhood on main traffic arteries,
without disturbing life within. Dudok thought that work had to
be performed with frugal means. 'In the art of town and village
planning, we architects usually realize too late that the most
pregnant effect is usually achieved … with what amounts to
nothing. At least with little of what is 'architecture' on our drawing
boards,' he wrote in 1927.
Dudok was to design countless working-class homes for the 25
municipal housing complexes which were constructed in Hilversum.
Pivotal for such a complex was either a library, a school, abattoir or
bathhouse. He also designed cemeteries, small parks and other
places with a civic function. As financial resources dwindled he was

forced to amalgamate the houses into bigger groups. This was especially true for the complexes located 'on the other side of the tracks', which were primarily conceived as working-class homes. After the Second World War, he would opt for multistorey construction, which meant that the height of the buildings increased and the village-like character was lost.

Dudok became increasingly interested in the landscape, especially when in 1923 he took a seat on the Centrale Schoonheidscommissie, a design review commission concerned with aesthetics, for the Gooi region, later even becoming its chairman. From the 1925 report that this commission drew up on the conservation of the natural beauty in the Gooi, it seems that they saw the city and the geographical space in which it was set as a single planning entity. The beauty of the Gooi was above all thanks to the woodland and heath. 'A factor of significance,' the commission stated, 'is the vastness of the natural areas, in such stark contrast to the beauty of works of art, for which it is exclusively a consideration of quality. For the beauty of a landscape, the quantitative aspect is undoubtedly of essential value. Woodland must be of such dimensions that one can have the sense of losing oneself in it, of being far away from the harriedness of everyday life. In order to flourish, a heath must be spacious, preferably stretching 'to infinity'; the undulating heath, stretching to the horizon and bounded only by blue sky and white clouds, has extraordinary significance in our turbulent existence. Where expansiveness and space exist, one should therefore do everything in order to preserve it.' It was obvious to Dudok that it would be impossible to call a halt to construction but, he maintained, the existing villages had to grow 'like flowers: orderly, rational, outward from a central point. All skulduggery in this respect is unacceptable. Thus, one ought to absolutely resist the creation of separate villa parks, existing outside any intimate relation to the village core. Such villa parks have frequently sprung up at the most beautiful locations, and have already fragmented the landscape all too severely.'

The recurring theme was 'how, while incurring as little loss of natural beauty as possible, to satisfy the demand for new living space?' Dudok argued that there needed to be a systematic and economical continuation of the building process, extending outward from the existing cores. Expansion plans would have to be succinct and rational, and a star-like development of the city resisted.

As an architect and town planner, Dudok believed that the primary concern with future expansions of existing towns would necessarily be the relationship between town and country. The distinction between them did not merely have to be obvious and acute, but they both had to be tackled as part of one and the same approach. He believed they were 'two values, town and country, entirely different, but complementing each other so beautifully, in the same way that in an harmonious building the vertical element can resonate with the horizontal.' These counterparts had to make their respective contributions in a harmonious way to contribute to a well-balanced whole. The compact silhouette of the town was one of Dudok's leading principles. That was what he wished to achieve or reinstate. Hilversum had to remain a large residential village with a maximum of 100,000 inhabitants and it could not have too great an impact on the surrounding natural beauty.

It goes without saying that Dudok had a traditional conception of the town, vested in family and community values. For him, the town was a place where one had to be able to feel at home and where a sense of beauty prevailed. That beauty had to have an educative and constructive quality, even if artificially designed. Imbuing a sense of security was a task for the architect. Dudok was not blind to developments in society, but he attached little value to them for the actual task of designing, in the knowledge that in the course of time the cards would fall differently once again. He was not ignorant of increasing mobility, but he was not prepared to design a town for which 'rapid movement' was the only guiding principle. He saw the town as a body with the core as its heart, and as such it also made systolic, diastolic and peristaltic movements. The neighbourhoods still largely function as Dudok had intended. It is true that the little streets are often blocked with parked cars and that the houses are perhaps too small by modern-day standards, but they are still neighbourhoods in which there is space for life on the street and where life still thrives on the street. In this, at least, the work of Dudok is of indisputable relevance and has a quality that endures as a guiding light.

1925-1930
Kiefhoek Rotterdam

1e Kiefhoekstraat
2e Kiefhoekstraat
Eemstein
Heer Arnoldstraat
H. Idoplein
H. Idostraat
Lindtstraat
Meerdervoortstraat
Nederhovenstraat

J.P. Oud **Housing Kiefhoek, 1925-1930 (photo 1930)**

The Kiefhoek stands out as an oddity against the surrounding buildings. To the right, the porch-access flats on the Groene Hilledijk, dating from the early twentieth century, at the top the buildings along the Hillevliet. Photograph taken from the southwest.

J.J.P. Oud **Kiefhoek, 1925-1930, corner solutions**

NAI collection, Oud archive

Sketches for corner options and perspectives show how J.J.P. Oud staged both an urban and a village setting.

J.J.P. Oud **Kiefhoek, 1925-1930, bird's-eye view from the northwest**

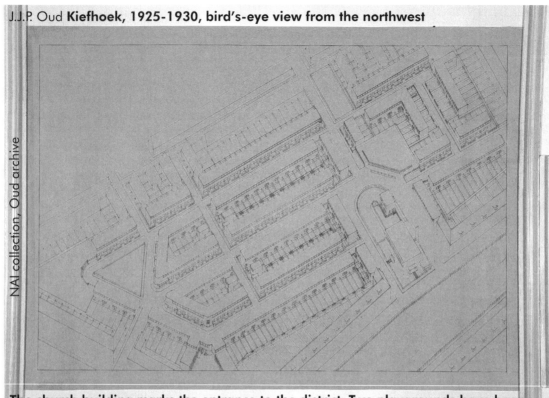

NAI collection, Oud archive

The church building marks the entrance to the district. Two playgrounds have been laid out for children.

J.J.P. Oud **Dwelling floorplan, normal type, 1925**

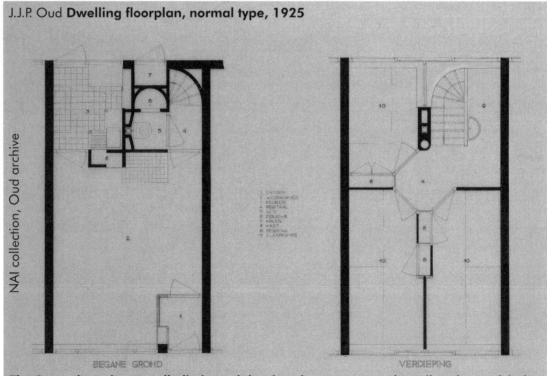

NAI collection, Oud archive

BEGANE GROND   VERDIEPING

The Rotterdam city council eliminated the tiny shower next to the toilet, the coal-hole and the folding ironing-board in the kitchen. These items were deemed 'unnecessary and excessive.'

"De Kiefhoek" R'dam.   Arch J Oud.

Behind the glass façade, next to Nederhovenstraat 19, is where the hot-water supply is located. On the first floor, behind the blind wall, is the storage. The sitting room and bedrooms are located behind and above the boiler room.

J.J.P. Oud **Heer Arnoldstraat, 1928-1930, sketch**

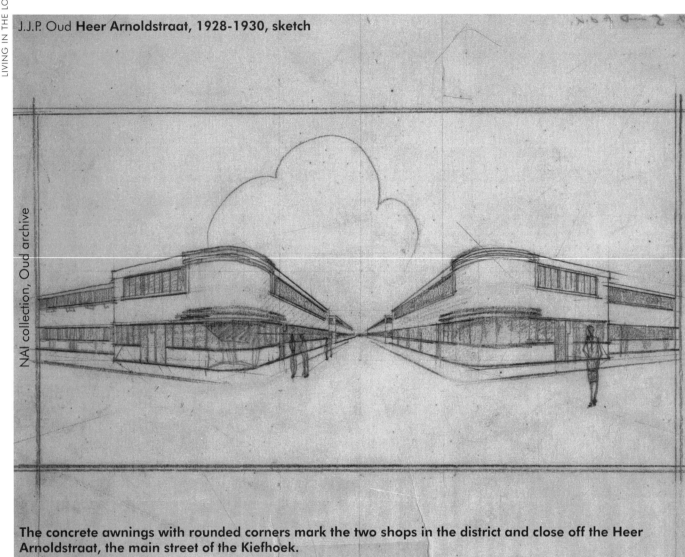

The concrete awnings with rounded corners mark the two shops in the district and close off the Heer Arnoldstraat, the main street of the Kiefhoek.

J.J.P. Oud **Shops on the Heer Arnoldstraat/Hendrik Idoplein, 1928-1930 (photo circa 1930)**

The only round shapes in the district are those of the shop buildings. They are an indication of modern production techniques and quickly became the emblem of the district.

J.J.P. Oud **Hendrik Idoplein, 1928-1930 (photo circa 1930)**

Kiefhoek is an integral design of dwellings and housing environment. The public garden on the Hendrik Idoplein is enclosed by a fence; on the corner a bench has been made part of the enclosure.

The 'Dwelling-Ford': cutting and contriving for 2,740 guilders per house
Martien de Vletter

The architect J.J.P. Oud (1890-1963) drew international attention with two exceptional housing construction projects. A diminutive row of houses in Hoek van Holland and a small neighbourhood in Rotterdam, the Kiefhoek, were shown alongside a few other designs at an important international exhibition in the Museum of Modern Art in New York in 1932. Photographs, plans and maquettes showed that Oud had a highly personal interpretation of the International Style and applied this in social-sector housing for blue-collar workers. There was a great deal of interest in the Kiefhoek project in particular, as the plan did not just consist of housing but also included a clear-cut urban plan which even allotted space for a church and other public amenities. Development of the Kiefhoek was the direct consequence of the area being declared unfit for habitation in 1925 and subsequent slum clearance. This exacerbated the shortage of housing for large families with a low income in this part of Rotterdam. Although Rotterdam's Woningdienst (Municipal Housing Agency), where Oud was employed, had already drafted an alarming report about this in the early 1920s, it took until 1926 before the first design for the Kiefhoek was presented to Rotterdam's council treasury committee. After a number of adaptations, the plan – the last, by the way, that Oud was to draft for the Housing Department – was specified in detail and ready for tender in 1928. The construction budget was 2,740 guilders per dwelling and the rent was set at 4.05 guilders per week. The last house was completed in 1930.
The complex consisted of 291 dwellings, two shops-cum-dwellings, a house with a water distillery and two small warehouses. The houses were fitted into a problematic, low-lying, triangular location in the Hillepolder. This area had already been subdivided into building lots in 1923 to an urban plan devised by the architect R.J. Hoogeveen. Thanks to a smart use of proportions, bevelled corners and indentations, Oud succeeded in transforming Hoogeveen's neutral and irregular street layout into the plan of an intimate village. Also, through an efficient use of space, he managed to design almost 300 properties without making use of upper and lower dwellings, as was the case elsewhere in the vicinity. From a town planning perspective, Oud attempted to couple the layout with a number of collective amenities, such as a church, playgrounds and a public garden. The inward-looking, village-like character was inventively underscored by the architec-tural detailing. The shops enliven the whole plan through their placement and their spacious, open architecture.
Most renowned is the symmetrical composition of the two rounded shop-front windows on either side of the central and most luxurious street; from the vantage point of the Groene Hilledijk they set off the village with a stunning entrance. Oud also endeavoured to compensate for the plan's irregularities by using symmetrical arrangements elsewhere in the design. For example, he built free-standing houses at the ends of the elongated housing blocks. As with other projects from this period, Oud was fixated on the effect of contrast between the enclosed interior courtyards and the open, long perspective of the street. The many sketches for corner solutions and perspectives demonstrate how to deliberately compose a town- or villagescape.

Oud succeeds in uniting a modern urban character and a rural character in this plan. The urban and modern is emphasized by the compact density, the standardized house types, the flat roofs and the grand town planning gestures – certainly when compared to the neighbouring Tuindorp Vreewijk garden suburb, which was designed by the Verhagen, Granpré Molière and Kok bureau.

The rural was encapsulated in the ground-hugging construction and the open spaces. The composition of the white-plastered, uniform facades relies mainly on three continuous strips stacked on top of one another. The eaves, bands of fenestration and the parapets underscore the horizontality of the elongated blocks of housing.

For Oud, the design of the Kiefhoek did not stop with the exterior. The whole design (the façade, the outdoor space, the street furniture and the interiors) it is clear that Oud took special care with the details. The normal type on which these houses are based was devised by Oud after extensive research. An efficient layout of the dwelling gains a maximum usable surface area.

In the first design for the Kiefhoek from 1925, the walls dividing the homes were to be realized in poured concrete and the outer walls in pre-cast concrete slabs. Building in concrete turned out to be more expensive than building in brick. Except for a number of prefabricated concrete elements (the foundation beams, the chimney flue and lintels), the blocks were built of brick and then faced in white plaster in order to give them a modern look.

The colour scheme is integral to the design, and the colours are inextricably linked with the composition of the façade. They reinforce the continuity and the rhythm in the clearly articulated street elevation. The colours are subservient to the architecture. They underscore the classical composition of the facade.

In 1930, even before the first houses for the Kiefhoek were realized, the plan for the layout of the plots and the floor plans were exhibited and discussed at the third Congrès Internationaux d'Architecture Moderne (CIAM) in Brussels. Oud subsequently published the project in various foreign periodicals, comparing his design to the designs of automobile manufacturer Henry Ford. In *The Studio* (1931), he wrote:

THE £ 213 HOUSE: A SOLUTION TO THE RE-HOUSING PROBLEM FOR ROCK-BOTTOM INCOMES IN ROTTERDAM BY ARCHITECT J.J.P. OUD

(…)

The problem for the architect was, accordingly, an interesting one. Its solution was found along the lines indicated by Henry Ford in his production of cars that were to be both good and cheap – namely, the practical construction and production methods, standardisation permitting of all components being factory-made, and economical organisation of space and material – 'Dwelling Fords', in fact.

Space does not permit of [sic] going into the technical details, but in general it may be said that the plan of the houses is as compact as possible with no room wasted on corridors. Also the design allowed for the use of either concrete or brick, according to prices ruling this materials, a factor which, in Holland, is largely affected by the demand. Equally, the maintenance of a good standard in joiners' work (apt otherwise to be degraded in mass-production) was ensured by designing the joinery items in relation to each other so that exactness of fit had unavoidably to be maintained.

Oddly enough, Oud only published his design for the Kiefhoek in foreign periodicals. It prompted a whole spectrum of reactions. At the CIAM it was seen as an example of rationalist housing construction. Hitchcock and Johnson from the United States, however, had misgivings about what they perceived as a manneristic architectural approach. J.B. van Loghem (1881-1940), usually one of Oud's detractors, was the first to publish a detailed and positive critique of the Kiefhoek in the Netherlands. Here he paid tribute to Oud for being the first person to have shown that the new architecture was not merely an expression of luxury, but that it was also perfectly feasible to build a modern working-class neighbourhood with limited means.

The area was thoroughly renovated in the 1990s. The houses no longer satisfied our modern-day requirements. It is exceptional that the character of the Kiefhoek has been preserved, even though the floor plans of the houses have been radically altered. Two houses were converted into one, though this is barely visible on the outside, while the public space was spruced up. The Kiefhoek still survives as an enclave within Rotterdam and there are still hundreds of architecture tourists who visit to photograph one of the highlights of Oud's oeuvre.

1940-1960
Middelburg

Gravenstraat
Groenmarkt
Grote Markt
Lange Delft

Centre of Middelburg, 1946 aerial photo

On 17 May 1940 part of the centre of Middelburg was destroyed by a German bombardment, because Zeeland refused to capitulate. The photo from 1946 shows that reconstruction has begun: the pattern of new streets is already visible. The historic ring around the centre, a holdover from the mound structure, was retained in the reconstruction. In the centre the town hall, on the right the abbey complex. Eschauzier's dwellings for the elderly have already been completed and look out onto the abbey.

P. Verhagen **Original situation and reconstruction plan, design 1940, completion 1946-1960**

Forum (1946) no. 1

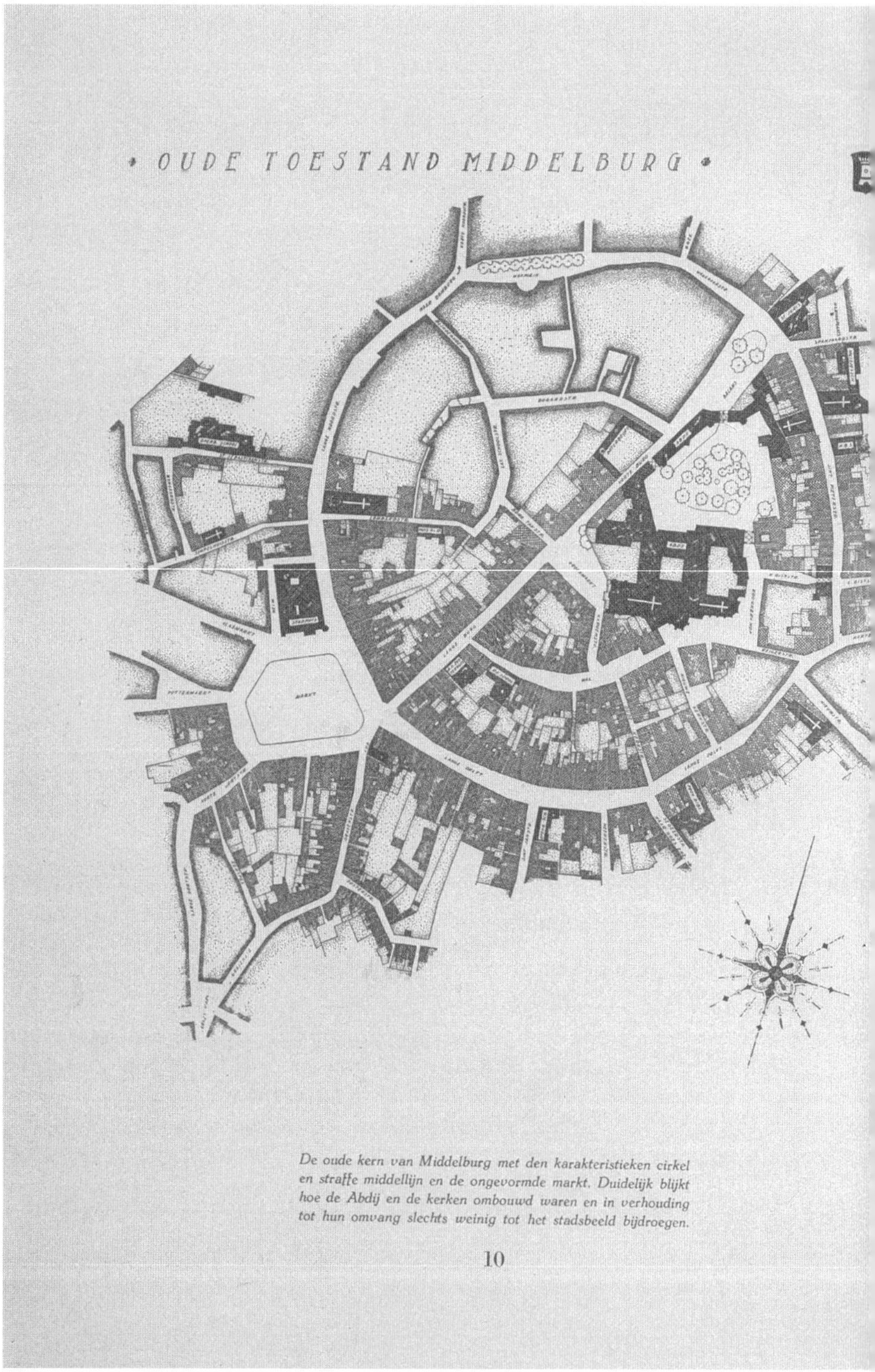

- OUDE TOESTAND MIDDELBURG -

De oude kern van Middelburg met den karakteristieken cirkel en straffe middellijn en de ongevormde markt. Duidelijk blijkt hoe de Abdij en de kerken ombouwd waren en in verhouding tot hun omvang slechts weinig tot het stadsbeeld bijdroegen.

10

The pre- and post-war situation of the centre of Middelburg. The straight line that divided the centre has been shifted, so that the landmark abbey now stands on its own. The shape of the square (left) in front of the town hall has also been changed,

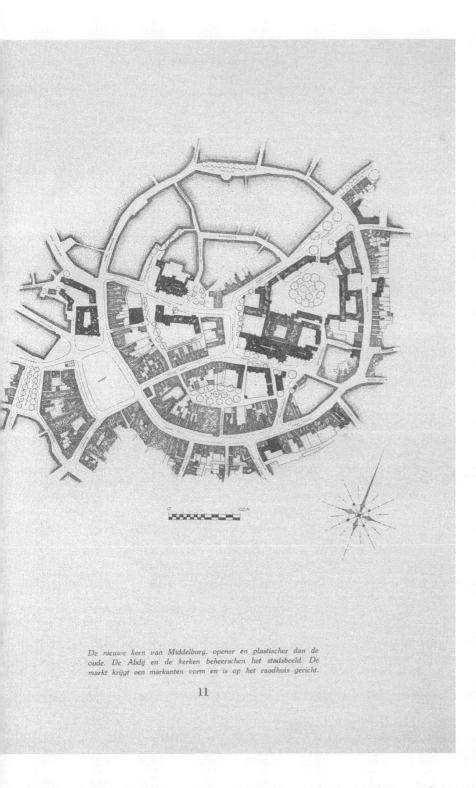

De nieuwe kern van Middelburg, opener en plastischer dan de oude. De Abdij en de kerken beheerschen het stadsbeeld. De markt krijgt een markanten vorm en is op het raadhuis gericht.

11

to make the town hall more prominent. Shot from the journal *Forum* from 1946, that published the very first article devoted to the reconstruction of Middelburg.

P. Verhagen **Façades, circa 1940**

The city of Rotterdam, bombarded on 10 May 1940, opted for the future. Bomb-damaged Middelburg turned back to its glorious past in urban planning and architecture.

: Eschauzier **Courtyard with dwellings for elderly people, 1941**

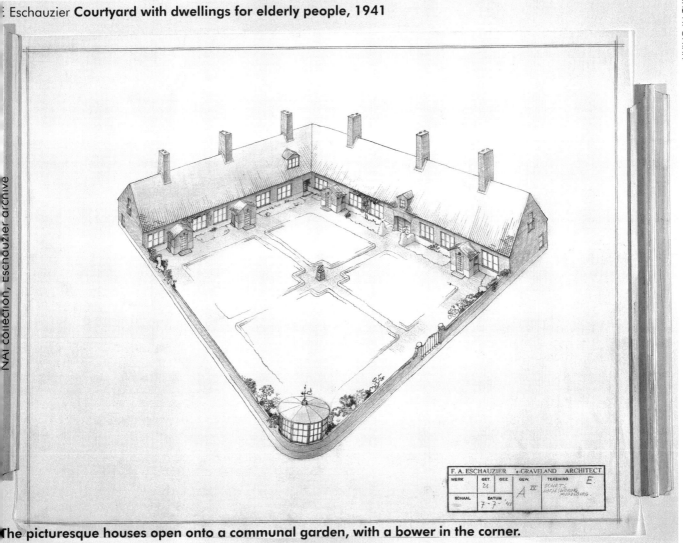

The picturesque houses open onto a communal garden, with a bower in the corner.

F. Eschauzier **Courtyard with dwellings for elderly people, 1941, façades**

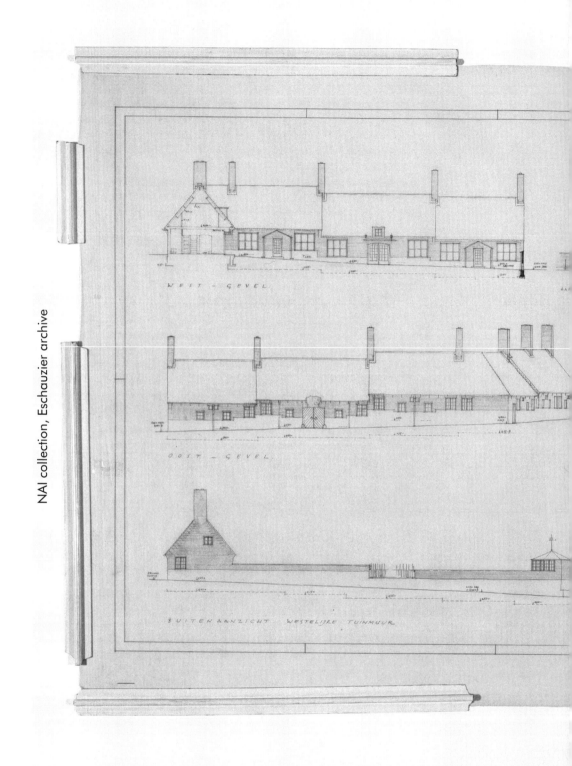

NAI collection, Eschauzier archive

The brick garden walls and the bower are part of the architectural whole.

WITHDRAWN-UNL

Grote Markt in the direction of the Lange Delft (photo circa 1955)

Zeeuws archive collection, Middelburg

Supervisor P. Verhagen did not want an exact copy of the old city, but rather strived for a 'characteristic Middelburg atmosphere.'

De Lange Delft (photo circa 1955)

Zeeuws archive collection, Middelburg

P. Verhagen also stipulated guidelines for the dimensions of windows and window-panel arrangements, by which he aimed to prevent shops being fitted with large, modern display windows.

Middelburg 1940: a new historic city centre
Marinke Steenhuis

The *Gids der voornaamste gemeenten van Nederland* ('Guide to the leading municipalities of the Netherlands') was published in 1929, the non plus ultra bookshelf reference for wealthy citizens looking for an attractive place to live. The guide lauded Middelburg as a 'true city for living', popular with tourists drawn by the handsome facades and traditional Zeeland costumes which could be admired at the market square every day. What the guide neglected to mention was that the former island of Walcheren and its centrally situated city of Middelburg had completely stagnated in economic terms. Middelburg owed its attractive image to its prosperity during the late Middle Ages, when, as a port on the approach to Bruges and Antwerp, the city had been part of the economic landscape of the Scheldt delta. In the seventeenth century, Middelburgwas the second Dutch India Company city of the Republic, after Amsterdam. Thereafter it went downhill: the population tumbled from 27,000 in 1675 to 12,500 in 1815. By the start of the twentieth century, all that remained to shore up the city's economy were the attractions mentioned in the guide: a pleasant living environment in an historic city centre, a marketplace for Walcheren and a tourist destination.

On 17 May 1940, only three days after the razing of Rotterdam, the centre of Middelburg was devastated by German bombs. Almost 600 properties in the city centre were destroyed, including many monuments: the Stadhuis (City Hall) in late-Gothic style overlooking the Markt marketplace, the Abdij (Abbey) complex of churches, the Provinciale Bibliotheek (Provincial Library), the Oost-Indisch Huis (East-India House, formerly the local headquarters of the Dutch East India Company) and the Botermarkt (Butter Market), a pre-eminent tourist attraction. The city had become an empty husk. It was immediately obvious that the city's prospects were severely restricted by the loss of these monuments. During recon-struction it was of the utmost importance to revivify the historic character of the city centre, in contrast to Rotterdam, which was on its way to a glorious future as an international port city. Middel-burg's future depended on its past.

One month after the bombardment, the town planner P. Verhagen (1882-1950) was appointed by the government commissioner J.A. Ringers as the designer for the reconstruction plan. Verhagen already had more than 100 expansion plans and regional plans to his name. He was selected primarily thanks to his winning submis-sion for the design competition for the clearance of Nijmegen's lower city (1939). A rubble clearance team had set to work imme-diately after the bombardment on Ringers's orders. The guiding principle for the reconstruction plan was the preser-vation of the typical ring-shaped plan, the architecture and the atmosphere of Middelburg. The mayor and aldermen even dared to hope 'that it shall be possible to present the various monumental buildings – especially the City Hall – to even better effect in the future than was the case in the past.'

Verhagen prized Middelburg's core for the combination of Gothic and Baroque in a single cityscape. In a 'wonderfully preserved Gothic street plan', the Abbey and the City Hall stood in the midst of street elevations with 18th-century townhouses. The typology of the cityscape consisted of small-scale circular and radial streets lined by towering, articulated walls. The existing valuable context of street layout and monuments that were luckily spared or to be rebuilt were, for Verhagen, the argument to make alterations to the street layout and make the construction subservient to the past, though without neglecting efficiency.

A crucial notion in Verhagen's explanation of the plan was the *rhythm* of Middelburg: the interaction between city plan, cityscape and scale. This stood its ground, according to Verhagen, against every form of monumentality. The rhythm sprang from the contrast with the landscape-related characteristics. In his *Toelichting bij het stedebouwkundig herbouwplan voor Middelburg* ('Explanation of the urban reconstruction plan for Middelburg') dated 9 September 1940, he gave the following graphic explanation: 'Most especially in Zeeland, where the landscape with its great dikes, the water with its broad and always troubled currents and the always so expansive skies with powerful clouds is of so massive a scale, the city is suited to the scale of mankind, and consequently small and enclosed, without pomp, though not without surprises. The preservation of these elements has resulted in this plan not being conceived in one great sweep, but sensitively. Carefully, with love and attention, the further elaboration will also initially be allowed to evolve sensitively, house by house, street by street.'

Within this endeavour to preserve the context, the city had to be readied for the future. That meant space for the market traffic, attractive routes for tourists and arterial roads to the various points of the compass. Verhagen repeatedly tested the required rational interventions in the city layout against the historic and symbolic programme. Besides the rhythm of the city, the concept of atmosphere played a key role here. Verhagen wanted to accentuate the contrast between the bustle and vivacity around the market and the peace and serenity around the Abbey by, as it were, evoking these busy and peaceful atmospheres. This resulted in the creation of a system of urban spaces that were attuned to Verhagen's analysis of the city down to the last detail.

The plan was primarily guided by five substantial functional interventions: the widening of the route from the Lange Delft to the outer ringroad, the addition of a green inner ring, the alteration of the straight Lange Burg – Korte Burg – Balans route into a bayonet form, the relocation of the market and the projection of two breakthroughs for arterial roads. Verhagen handled his proposals based on the urban functions of living, working, relaxation and traffic. The mansions were allocated for residential functions; employment was concentrated around the main shopping street and the Markt. City-centre recreation was to be found in the green inner ring. Traffic, according to Verhagen in the *Toelichting* already quoted above, '... was indeed not taken into account by the old Gothic practitioners, and we have been obliged to reorganize this, but even those transformations will exceed expectations.'

Nine functions, ranging from houses to shops, cafés and gardens had been allotted a place in the city, completely in harmony with the desired atmosphere at each locale. Cafés, restaurants and shops were to be set around the southern half of the Markt, while around the City Hall and Abbey – to preserve the calm – only offices and housing were planned. Hotels could be established overlooking the Markt opposite the city hall and on the enlarged Groenmarkt (Vegetable Market) opposite the abbey. The city's guests had to be received in the most beautiful salons. The actual realization of the city as a whole, as a unified entity, as Verhagen wanted, was far from simple. The biggest stumbling block was the reorganization of the building lots. Former owners were indignant because the new zoning plan meant they could not return to their original address and had to negotiate for a lot elsewhere.

Reconstruction of the city centre began in 1941, following a system of groups of six properties at once, in an attempt to retain the individuality of each property. Verhagen wanted the architecture to correspond with the great ceiling height and the imposing scale of the old 18th-century merchants' townhouses. In order to work as an architect in Middelburg, the most important criterion was the preparedness to adapt to the city's typical atmosphere. Verhagen emphasized that his directions only applied where the lively Flemish architecture set the tone of the city's appearance; the architects had to make their own originality the lowest priority 'with seemingly anonymous work'. For him the important thing was not to imitate stylized features, but the overall lines, the vertical impact of the individual facades and maintaining Middelburg's typology, which for him were couched in terms like scale, compo-sition, rhythm, colour and materials. For Verhagen these were self-evident concepts that he presented to the architects like a toolbox for the design task. However, the abstractions proved difficult for architects to translate into a concrete design. The creation of a contemporary gable within a complex of contextual restrictions often produced little more than straitjacketed attempts. In short, it seems that Verhagen's quest for a distinctive Middelburg style was not achieved – something that he himself had already admitted in 1942 and which drew criticism after the liberation. Moreover, at that point only 46 properties had been restored. Besides the archi-tecture, the planting scheme was of the highest importance for Verhagen. He invited the agricultural engineer G.A. Overdijkink, a forester for Staatsbosbeheer (the Dutch forestry commission) in Utrecht to draft a design. The predominance of the common linden, an ideal city tree, was intended to reinforce the unity of the cityscape.

Within the functional demands of traffic, living and commerce, Verhagen strove to create a modern city on the basis of an old typology. The urban plan was an unsullied translation of the programme: historical value, tourism and traffic.

Criticism of the reconstruction of Middelburg now seems to be a thing of the past. In 1975, the Year of Monuments, Middelburg was singled out as an exemplary city in which new construction had not detracted from the identity of the extant. Verhagen had based his reconstruction plan on the character of the extant. That argument no longer seems necessary. Complete historic city centres are mushrooming as new construction projects in the meadows.

1947-1965
Pendrecht/Alexanderpolder Rotterdam

area in between
Groene Kruisweg
harbour railway line
Oldegaarde
Zuiderparkweg

One of the first sketches by L. Stam-Beese in which the principle of the residential cluster was elaborated. The separation between traffic arteries and dead-end 'residential streets' is clearly visible.

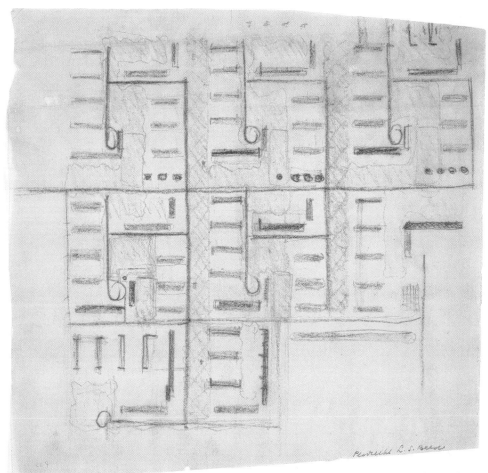

L. Stam-Beese / Urban Development and Reconstruction Department **Pendrecht expansion plan, 1947-1951; completion 1953-1960, detail with residential clusters**

L. Stam-Beese / Urban Development and Reconstruction Department **Pendrecht expansion plan, 1947-1951; completion 1953-1960, view of district centre from the southeast**

NAI collection, Stam-Beese archive

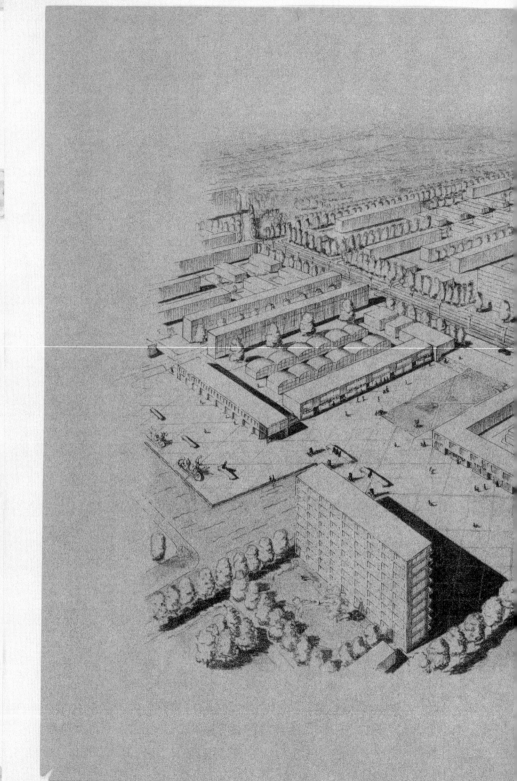

View of the district centre (which would later become Plein 1953) with at bottom right a covered swimming pool with an outside pool, and further along the square's shop galleries with commercial spaces behind them. At top right a connecting strip of

community facilities (churches, schools) can be made out, closed off by a high-rise, which would become W. Wissing's **HAL** building.

J. Bakema / Opbouw **Plan Pendrecht I for CIAM 7 (Bergamo), 1949, residential cluster**

NAI collection, Van den Broek en Bakema archive

With a series of three maquettes, Opbouw demonstrated Pendrecht as a model of modern urban planning, based on the systematic repetition of the residential cluster. Within this cluster, high-rises, low-rises and walk-up flats are combined.

J. Bakema / Opbouw **Plan Pendrecht I voor CIAM 7 (Bergamo), 1949, neighbourhood**

NAI collection, Van den Broek en Bakema archive

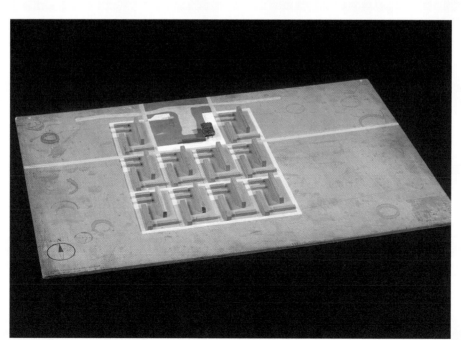

Ten housing clusters are combined into a neighbourhood. The neighbourhood centre, a park with school, community centre and a block of flats, is situated on the edge, linked to the communal greenbelt.

J. Bakema / Opbouw **Plan Pendrecht I for CIAM 7 (Bergamo), 1949, district**

NAI collection, Van den Broek en Bakema archive

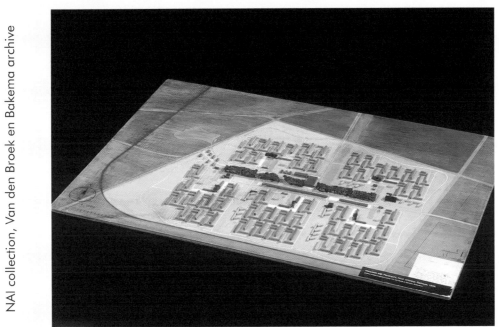

The entire area, consisting of four neighbourhoods of eight to 10 residential clusters. Area facilities are concentrated in a centrally situated centre and a greenbelt running north to south, with schools, a medical centre and offices.

J. Bakema / Opbouw **Plan Pendrecht II for CIAM 8 (Hoddesdon), 1951, district**

NAI collection, Van den Broek en Bakema archive

The most significant criticism of the first Pendrecht plan was that it was based too much on repetition and was not sufficiently urban. By means of larger residential clusters and a larger centre, the plan acquired greater clarity and scale.

J. Bakema **Plan Pendrecht II for CIAM 8 (Hoddesdon), 1951, district**

NAI collection, Van den Broek en Bakema archive

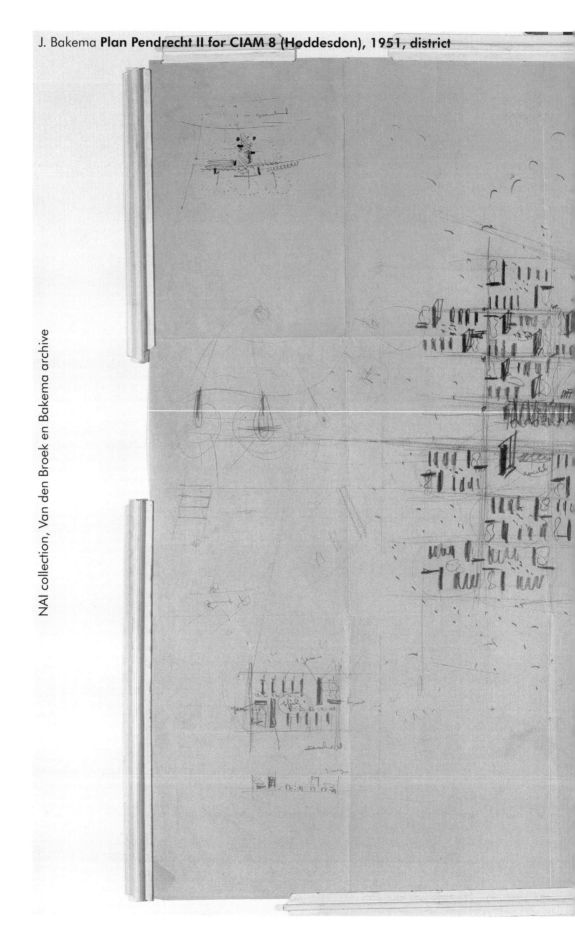

In this sketch, Bakema shifts the emphasis of the housing clusters and neighbourhoods to the collective amenities. These are concentrated in a large structure in the shape of windmill sails, accented by several high-rise flat buildings. This turns the entire plan into a dynamic whole instead of an accumulation of residential districts.

J. Bakema / Opbouw **Plan Alexanderpolder for CIAM 9 (Aix-en-Provence 1953), situation and details**

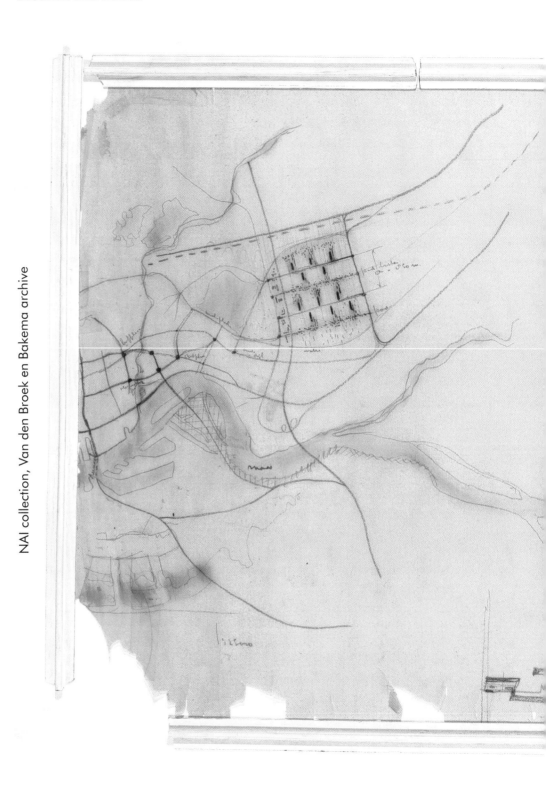

NAI collection, Van den Broek en Bakema archive

The new, larger scale Bakema introduced with his 'mammoth' – vertical residential communities for thousands of people – especially the high-rises, was the subject of controversy within the Dutch CIAM group. The area consists of 11 vertical residential communities lining access roads that follow the polder parcel allotments.

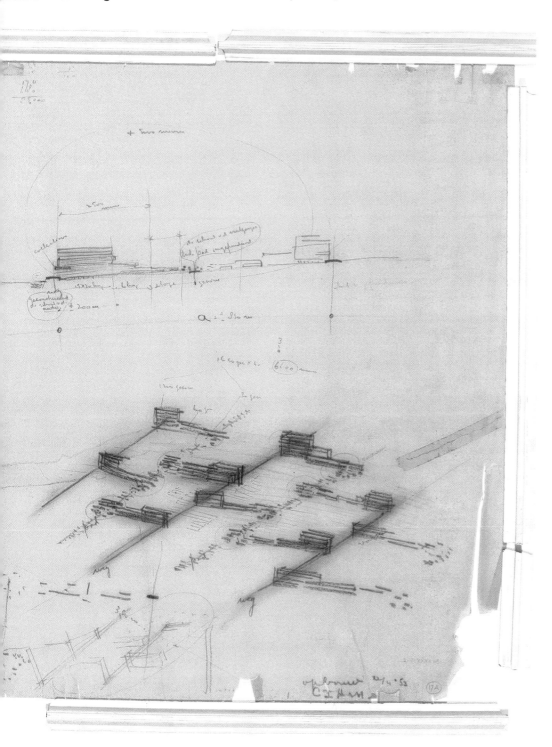

74681

VERDELING DER WOONVORMEN VOLGENS GEZINSSAMENSTELLING DER ROTTERDAMSE BEVOLKING.	BEGANE GROND	VERDIEPING.	HOOGBOUW.
ALLEENSTAANDE PERSONEN 3%			3%
OUDEN VAN DAGEN. 6⁵%	6⁵%		
48%		40%	8%
20⁵%	9%	11⁵%	
EN MEER 22%	22%		
ANALYTISCHE SAMENSTELLING :	37⁵%	51⁵%	11%
GEPROJECTEERD :	38%	52⁵%	8⁵%

NAI collection, Stam-Beese archive

Schedule attuned to population composition and needed housing types within the residential cluster

L. Stam-Beese / Urban Development and Reconstruction Department **Pendrecht expansion plan, 1947-1951; completion 1953-1960, view from the east between tussen Oldegaarde (right) and Slinge (left) (1958 photo)**

NAI collection, Stam-Beese archive

Woningen in Pendrecht, uit de lucht gezien in april 1958 (Aero-photo ,,Nederland").

At the top the first Pendrecht I neighbourhood. Below it a strip of greenery with a few schools and all the way to the right the HAL building under construction. This strip connects to the yet-to-be-realized Plein 1953 in the upper left corner. At bottom right is Pendrecht II, with the 'mirrored' residential clusters – built in symmetrical pairs – clearly recognizable. To the left is Pendrecht III, separated from Pendrecht II by a strip of smaller buildings (with gable roofs).

W. Wissing **Tower block for Holland Amerika Lijn, Oldegaarde, 1957-1960, façade (1960 photo)**

NAI collection, Wissing archive

94681

High-rises, a new form of housing at the time, were only implemented in a few places as an aethetic accent. This building with 81 dwellings in nine levels was built by W. Wissing for the Holland Amerika Lijn shipping line, and had such luxury accommodations as central heating, a central antenna for television and radio and a roof terrace.

NAI collection, Stam-Beese archive

The intimacy of the green inner area was perfectly suited for children. In the background, gallery flats with garages underneath – a new housing type for the time, a result of the unexpectedly rapid increase in demand for garages.

Rotterdam Public Housing Department **Research report, 'Residents' experience of the openness as well as the privacy of their dwellings and gardens', 1959, interior of a single-family dwelling in Pendrecht (1959 photo)**

NAI library collection

The photos certainly show no average interiours, but rather exude the ambiance of the model houses of Stichting Goed Wonen ('Good Housing Foundation') published in the magazine Goed Wonen.

Rotterdam Public Housing Department **Research report, 'Residents' experience of the openness as well as the privacy of their dwellings and gardens', 1959, interior of a single-family dwelling in Pendrecht (1959 photo)**

NAI library collection

This propaganda for a new housing culture, based on light, air and space, was influential, though research showed residents preferred security over openness and 'looking-in'.

Model for a new society
Jean-Paul Baeten

The Rotterdam district of Pendrecht was built within easy reach of the new Waalhaven docks for the workers employed there. It was a model development, born of the broadly supported post-war desire for a new, harmonious society. It is no coincidence that this experiment was conducted in Rotterdam, a symbol of the optimism and decisiveness of post-war reconstruction.

After the war, a great number of homes had to be built in Rotterdam in quick tempo. The housing stock in the new centre was drastically reduced. In addition, an explosive growth in port activities caused an influx of workers from the provinces. How to prevent the development of a chaotic, unending sea of houses as in the pre-war city, one in which the many newcomers would certainly feel lost? How could a new sense of community emerge from the anonymity of city life? The problem – but perhaps also its resolution – is still topical today.

The answer was sought in the neighbourhood and district structure that was also already a feature of the old city. For the post-war expansions, the choice fell on a decentralized city composed of more or less independent districts with about 20,000 residents, which were in turn subdivided into neighbourhoods. The district offered the city-dweller a clearly organized and intelligible living environment. District and neighbourhood centres for each area were supposed to reinforce the community spirit. This 'neighbourhood concept' was tested out in practice in Pendrecht. Busloads of architects from around the world came to see this 'prototype of modern living'.

The neighbourhood concept had already been developed in Rotterdam during the war by the Bos committee, which was named after its chairman, A. Bos, also director of the city's Public Housing Agency. The committee had ten members, from education, health-care and the churches. The only architect was W. van Tijen. In 1946, Bos published the findings in the report 'De stad der toekomst, de toekomst der stad' ('The city of the future, the future of the city'), advocating the neighbourhood concept as the basis for Rotterdam's future urban expansion. It was a model for social management as well as for urban planning, with the building of community along with social and cultural emancipation as its key goals. An important source of inspiration was post-Revolution Russia; several of the commission's members were socialists.

The underlying principle was a decentralized city model, inspired by the garden city concept, which was a composed of more or less autonomous units, the districts, each with a specific character and its own centre. Because of the limited size of the districts (a maximum of 20,000 residents), socially mixed neighbourhoods and adequate neighbourhood and district amenities, the community spirit among residents would be stimulated. Thanks to the neighbourhood-district-borough-city hierarchy, the anonymous urban space was shaped into a series of recognizable places. In contrast to the garden city, the neighbourhood concept was not anti-urban: the neighbourhoods were conceived as integral components of the city and were meant to convey a positive experience of urbanity through a gradual transition from small to large.

A practical advantage was that no time had to be wasted on a detailed 'general expansion plan' as in Amsterdam, so reconstruction of the city centre could begin immediately. The sites for the expansion districts was all that had to be decided; then they could be elaborated as required as independent entities. In the 1949 expansion plan for the Linker-Maasoever (the southern bank of the river Maas), the preference was for expansion in a southerly direction, close to the new docks, since the majority of the population worked there. The existing city ended here in a parkland belt, the Zuiderpark, to which three residential districts were linked – Zuidwijk, Pendrecht and Lombardijen – in turn separated from each other by green corridors. The design of these expansion areas corresponded with the garden-city character of the first expansion plan for Zuid (southern Rotterdam) by Verhagen, Granpré Molière and Kok dating from 25 years earlier.

In 1948, Lotte Stam-Beese (1903-1988), a town planner for Rotterdam's Department of Urban Development, was commissioned to design the westernmost district, Pendrecht. The number of inhabitants was set at 20,000 maximum, in keeping with the neighbourhood concept, and the construction density was set at 56 dwellings per hectare. The expected demography of the population was ascertained on the basis of research. Owing to the scarcity of materials and the productive urge of the reconstruction era, it was not only the floor plan of the houses that was tied to precise specifications, but also the amount of land per house type – the terreinindex – an index for the size of lots imposed by central government. Stam-Beese was faced with the difficult task of reconciling the high density of this restrictive programme with the ideals of the neighbourhood concept.

Stam-Beese, who had trained at the Bauhaus in the 1920s, was familiar with the international functionalist avant-garde. In her work as a town planner before the war, she already had plenty of practical experience with town planning according to the principles of the Congrès Internationaux d'Architecture Moderne (CIAM): open-row layouts and the separation of functions. From 1932 to 1934, for instance, she worked with Mart Stam (1899-1986) and Ernst May (1886-1970) in the USSR on the planning of a number of new cities. After the war she became a member of the revived Rotterdam-based Opbouw, a group of functionalist architects that was effectively the Dutch arm of the CIAM (along with De 8 – 'The Eight', its Amsterdam-based counterpart), together with Bakema, Hovens Greve, Wissing, Van Tijen, Van den Broek, Oud, Maaskant and others. Also employed by the city council were Bakema (who worked for the housing agency until 1949) and Hovens Greve, resulting in the unique situation that the CIAM avant-garde was in direct contact with practical town planning in Rotterdam.

Prompted by the commission for Pendrecht, the Opbouw architects decided to draft their own study design based on the same specifications as a submission for the sixth CIAM congress in Bergamo (1949). Stam-Beese could now directly gauge the discussions and design alternatives which had arisen within Opbouw against the real-life situation. A new design concept was born in Opbouw's laboratory situation that would give a completely new shape to the neighbourhood concept: the residential cluster.

The pre-war CIAM had primarily focused on achieving optimum housing efficiency through standardization, open-row layouts and the separation of functions and housing types, of high- and

low-rise. Opbouw now sought a spatial translation of the neighbourhood concept by juxtaposing different housing types. The
objective was a balanced distribution of all sections of the population and thus social cohesion. The residential cluster was an urban
planning concept as well as a social construct, a repeatable
framework of different residential blocks, which simultaneously
formed a social and formal unit and in which different family types
could be accommodated. It was theoretically both the smallest unit
within which a complete urban residential programme could be
realized and the biggest unit which residents could still experience
as a collective, as a community. It was 'that section of the whole city
which the resident can still survey as a single entity and with which
he still feels directly connected; not because it is more personal, but
due to the character and standing of the whole.'

In principle the residents could spend an entire domestic career –
from birth to old age – within the one cluster, which would promote
the social cohesion. The original residential cluster consisted of two
rows of three- and four-storey apartment buildings for smaller
families and single people, and three rows of low-rise construction
of one and two storeys for large families and the aged set around a
communal garden. The cluster contained 90 units on a surface area
measuring 80x140 metres: a density of 56 units per hectare. Six to
eight clusters constituted a neighbourhood; four neighbourhoods
constituted a district. In spite of the necessarily high building density
it was still possible to create considerable spaciousness by combining
the different forms of housing, making gardens communal wherever
possible, and by partially replacing streets with pathways.

The most important difference between the theoretical model
developed by Opbouw and the executed design by Stam-Beese,
approved in October 1949, was that Stam-Beese mirrored the
housing clusters in symmetrical pairs. This reduced the emphasis on
the autonomous individual cluster and created a subtle alternation
of main roads, residential streets and pathways. Now, rather than a
series of similar elements, it created a more urban whole.

The effect of a continuous yet differentiated space, which simultaneously evoked cosy security and urban grandiosity, was crucial for
Stam-Beese: 'The open-air space bathes the blocks in such a way
as to achieve an effect of the block standing in space instead of the
block as the boundary of the space.' In this treatment of space, as
well as in the actual form of the housing unit, one can clearly detect
the influence of De Stijl, especially the architectural experiments of
Theo van Doesburg (1883-1931) and Cornelis van Eesteren (1897-
1988). Just like De Stijl, Stam-Beese's ultimate goal was a cohesive,
multidisciplinary Gesamtkunstwerk, a 'total work of art' which
extended to the interiors and would 'uplift' the residents. She
maintained contacts with the Stichting Goed Wonen ('Ideal Home
Foundation'), which promoted the 'sensible' interior for public
housing – open and spacious with soundly designed industrial
products – following on from the aesthetics of districts like
Pendrecht. Such paternalism had, moreover, an established place
in Dutch modernism.

The district amenities (schools, churches, district and community
centres, business space) were not integrated within the cluster, but
stood in a central green strip running north-south which separated
the neighbourhoods from one another. In an east-west direction the
neighbourhoods were divided by a broad access road (partly still
retaining the original ribbon development!) with a watercourse,

along which the shops were arranged. In the centre of the district, at the junction of the roadway and the band of greenery, there was a large pedestrian square with shops and civic buildings, the later Plein 1953. Additionally, blocks of flats were built at various landmark points.

The design from 1953 was realized almost exactly according to plan. The urban form was so compelling (Van Tijen even called the plan dictatorial) that substantial deviations were impossible and small variations did not affect the overall impression. The neighbourhoods were realized by different housing corporations. Each denominational 'pillar' had its own neighbourhood, recognizable from subtle architectural variations. In the Catholic neighbourhood, brick and pitched roofs prevailed. The socialist corporation elected for lots of glass and flat roofs, and propagated the 'Ideal Home' interior. In addition, there were entire streets and blocks of flats built by companies for their employees, for example the HAL flats, the Shell flats and the BP flats.

Pendrecht developed into a desirable residential area, cherished for the peace and quiet and the greenery, as well as for the high level of domestic comfort by standards of that time. The new community spirit, however, demanded more patience, even though the residents were proud of their neighbourhood. Sociological research in Pendrecht in 1958 indicated that the residential cluster was not experienced as a social unit; the composition of the population was too diverse and the intermingling too artificial. Though the openness and communal greenery were highly valued, the low-rise residents in particular complained about people looking in and a lack of privacy.

The neighbourhood concept was imitated everywhere in the initial post-war years, especially because it offered the possibility of accommodating the Dutch denominational and political 'pillars'. In addition, it complied with a desire shared by all political parties for a new societal organization. As a working model, thanks to the combination of clearly organized design principles and social objectives it was in harmony with the practical climate of the reconstruction era. But the idealistic objective, the fostering of a new sense of community, was nowhere to be found, since the denominational pillars were retained and no new socio-cultural institutions were established. By establishing neighbourhood councils, Rotterdam was alone, moreover, in also deriving administrative consequences from the model.

What did endure was the urban planning translation of the neighbourhood concept. The Pendrecht model with its differentiation between arterial roads and quiet residential streets and pathways, the intimate collective greenery and the varied housing stock would continue to determine the look of many expansion districts in the Netherlands until 1980.

In the meantime, the formulation of ideas within Opbouw about Pendrecht as a theoretical model continued. In 1949 and 1951, the plan was presented at various stages of development at the CIAM congresses in Bergamo and Hoddesdon. There it received much admiration, thanks to the consistent elaboration of urban living issues. The main criticism of the plan, already under construction, was the overly limited scale of the residential cluster and the lack of urbanity. In the design for the following congress in Hoddesdon, the residential clusters were enlarged and the level of amenities at the neighbourhood centre was also increased with, for example, day nurseries and blocks of flats for workers in specific industries.

When it became clear that Stam-Beese's model would be realized, attention shifted to another expansion area: the Alexanderpolder. In the studies for this district, the intimacy and security of the residential cluster was increasingly exchanged for the large-scale urbanity, which also tallied with the increasing scale of the post-war expansion areas. High-rise played an increasingly important role – albeit a constant point of controversy – and Bakema in particular ventured to use clusters, a completely new urban dimension, with his 'mammoths', which in fact formed vertical residential clusters. Here the enclosed social space of the residential cluster was exchanged for the 'total space' of the polder landscape. The eventual choice was a compromise, and the high-rise construction was integrated in residential clusters. This plan was also presented in the CIAM forum, while at the E55 fair it was presented to the people of Rotterdam as a maquette of the 'residential neighbour-hood of the future' measuring 15x15 metres. This formed the basis for Ommoord and Zevenkamp, dubbed 'Rotterdam's Bijlmer'.

1947-1956
Nagele

Akkerstraat
Eggestraat
Gerstehof
Hakstraat
Karwijhof
Klaverhof
Koolzaadhof
Lucernehof
Nagelersweg
Noorderdwarsstraat
Noorderlaan
Noorderpoort
Ploegstraat
Ring
Tarwehof
Vlashof
Voorhof
Voorhof
Zuiderachterstraat
Zuiderwinkels
Zuidwesterring

. van Gasteren **Documentary, 'Een nieuw dorp op nieuw land', 1959**

n 1959, filmmaker L. van Gasteren made the documentary 'Een nieuw dorp op nieuw land' ('A new village n new land'), about the process of creating Nagele. During filming, the architects and urban planners liscuss their plans. Against the back wall, the maquette of the definitive design of Nagele.

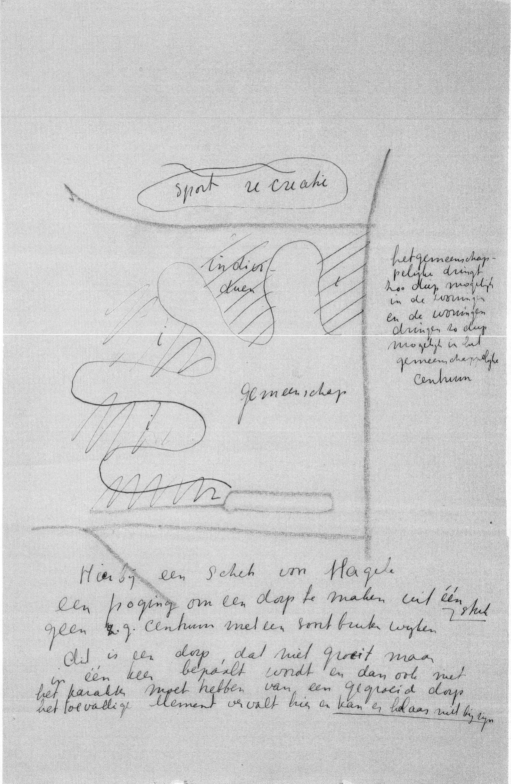

'Hereby a sketch for Nagele, an attempt to create a village as one unit. No so-called centre with some sort of suburbs. This is a village that does not grow but rather is delineated in one go, and thus must not have the character of a village that has grown. The element of chance is eliminated here.' G. Th. Rietveld, April 1948.

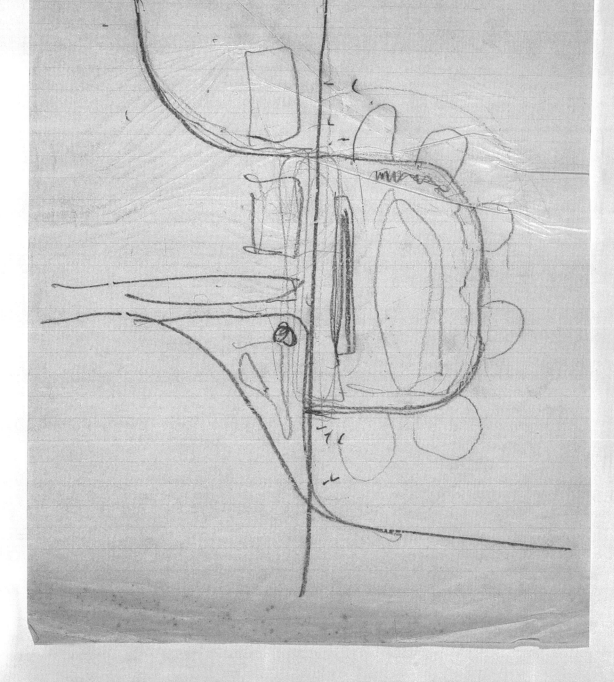

ayout of the traffic structure for Nagele by C. van Eesteren. The central traffic artery is situated west of the entre. A ring road borders the large central area and provides access to the residential sections, here still roposed as 'lobes'. The roadway structure was implemented in this way in the definitive plan.

M. Kamerling **Design for Nagele, 1947-1954, plan**

NAI collection, Kamerling archive

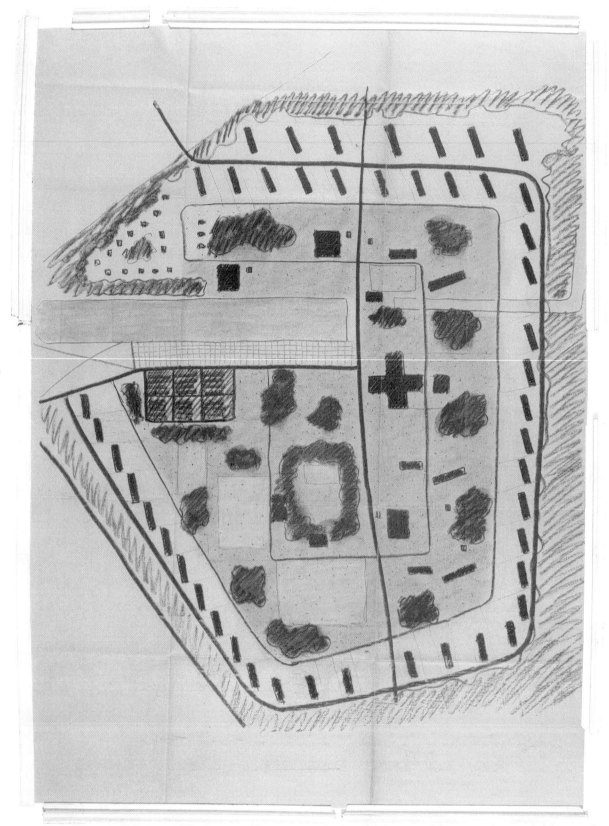

Early urban plan by M. Kamerling. The traffic artery, along which amenities are situated, bisects the centre. Medium-rise buildings are located in strips around the village like a shell.

Nagele   1 2000

de 8

Urban planning design by A. van Eyck, which was implemented in broad outline. The traffic artery runs alongside the village; the residential sections are situated around a large, open central area. The village is encircled by a wooded border, just as a farm on open land is sheltered from the wind by a screen of trees.

J. Niegeman and F. van Gool **Karwijhof middle-class dwellings, 1953-1954, floorplans, façades and cross-section**

NAI collection, Niegeman archive

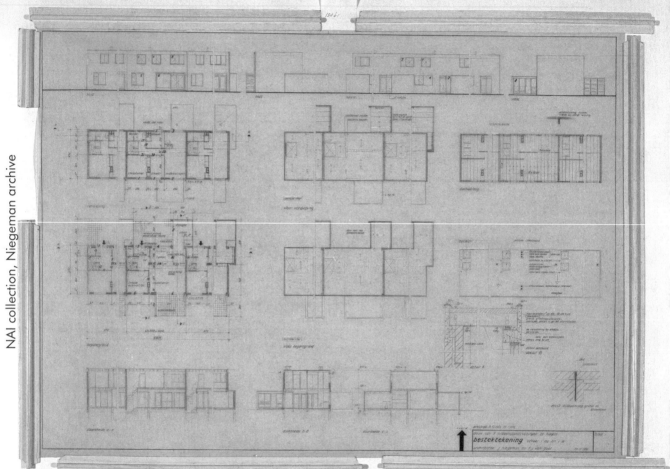

The dwellings with separate kitchen, sitting room, bedrooms and bathroom and toilet facilities are 'a wonder of comfort and modernity' for many. An open-plan sitting room-kitchen was proscribed, in order to let farm workers get used to urban cultural patterns.

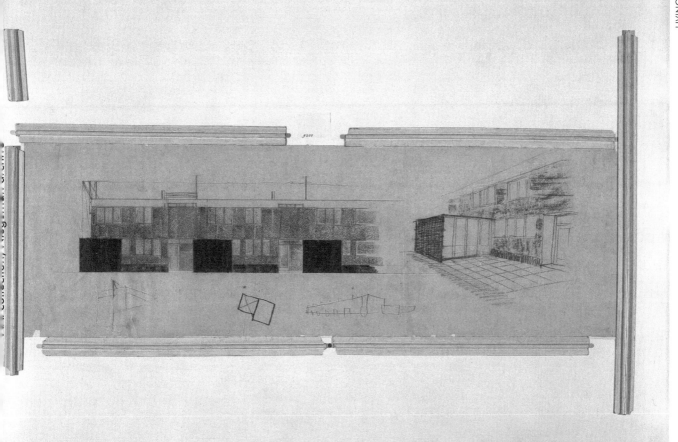

Niegeman and F. van Gool **Karwijhof middle-class dwellings, 1953-1954, façade drawing and perspective**

Nagele features only dwellings with individual front doors at the street level, no porch-access buildings or apartment blocks. This is a concession to the agricultural background of most residents.

Nagele housing construction, 1954-1956 (1958 photo)

State archive in Flevoland, photo archive

The mechanization of agriculture, changing operational methods and the new, precisely parcelled polder meant the end of romantic farm life.

Nagele housing construction, 1954-1956 (1958 photo)

State archive in Flevoland, photo archive

The neighbourhoods consist of strips of low-rise constructions, around a central grass field. This is the implementation of the 'neighbourhood principle' at a village level.

Nagele: a modern village for farm workers
Ellen Smit

At first glance, the farm workers' village of Nagele seems more like a post-war suburb of a Dutch city than a small-scale village in an agricultural area. Nagele is indeed the concrete embodiment of urban planning principles which, between 1945 and 1960, formed the basis for the design of post-war residential districts. These districts, such as Pendrecht and Zuidwijk in Rotterdam, were organized according to the 'neighbourhood principle', provided with shops and upholding a distinction between the four urban functions of housing, work, traffic and recreation. The village of Nagele was built in strict accordance with this organizational principle. The four urban functions are separated from each other, and each has been given a clear-cut place in the village. Traffic is kept out of the village by positioning the centre and the surrounding housing groups to the east of the north-south main road. The central area is a pedestrian zone, an open and green space where the churches and three schools are found. On the west side, the shops stand in an extended strip along the main road. Around the centre there are seven little residential clusters, equidistant from the centre so that the shops are within easy reach for everyone. The housing consists of rows of low-rise with flat roofs.

This town planning structure distinguishes Nagele from the other villages for agricultural workers in the Noordoostpolder, on the recently reclaimed land of the young province of Flevoland. These villages were created in the spirit of the architect M.J. Granpré Molière (1883-1972) and deliberately situated at road intersections, with a central village green surrounded by the village hall, churches and schools. Brick-built houses with pitched roofs were built along the main roads. Modernists like C. van Eesteren (1897-1988) and B. Merkelbach (1901-1961) dismissed these villages as a hackneyed idyll, but even for the project's commissioner, the 'Directie van de Wieringermeer' (the authority responsible for development of the Noordoostpolder), there were also doubts about whether all the villages should be built according to this traditional formula. For instance, A.D. van Eck, who supervised the various village plans for the authorities, saw little in the 'old finish' by Granpré Molière and thought that his romantic formal fripperies sat uncomfortably in midst of mechanized agriculture. He was strongly in favour of proceeding with the modernist group of Amsterdam architects, De 8. In late 1946, De 8, later joined by the counterpart Rotterdam architects' association Opbouw, was offered the opportunity to make a design for the village of Nagele. Though Nagele could be characterized as a post-war residential development, it was also designed as a village for agricultural workers, with low-rise houses equipped with kitchen gardens and chicken coops. During the design process for Nagele, discussions were not just about the desired modernity of the village, but also about the typical domestic culture of the agricultural workers and changes in rural society. This amalgamation of respect for the polder lifestyle and modern urban planning principles was described by G. Rietveld (1888-1964), one of more than 30 designers who worked on Nagele, in 1953: 'Everyone lives in a village rather than in a suburb; in personal freedom with the advantage and the shelter of the community. Give [the residents] a small taste of the big city in the village as well and they will feel more at home, and less hidebound.'

The majority of the population consisted of the agricultural workers' families, but there were also middle-class residents and people from the upper echelons of society living in the village. The houses in Nagele are arranged in seven groups around a green 'courtyard', constituting an application of the 'residential cluster' idea. In the post-war residential areas of large cities this consists of a combination of different housing types in low-, medium- and high-rise, grouped in a rectangular structure around a communal green space. However, there was no multi-storey or high-rise construction used in Nagele in response to an agricultural tradition of 'living on the land'. The small clusters consist of low-rise rows of terraced single-family dwellings arranged around a central lawn. These residential clusters housed agricultural labourers and the middle classes of every Christian denomination in separate rows, with the goal of advancing social cohesion among them.

The design of the houses was influenced by a tension between the 'gentrification offensive' aimed at the farm worker on the one hand, and respecting agricultural practices such as keeping chickens and growing potatoes on the other. The gentrification offensive resulted in all the houses being comfortable and modern for the time, though they were built frugally because of limited financial means. If one reflects that farm labourers were previously housed much more primitively, then the houses in Nagele with a separate kitchen, living room, bedrooms and sanitary facilities were 'a wonder of comfort and modernity'. The designers consciously avoided using a farm-like kitchen-cum-living-room in Nagele. The farm worker was thus forced to live in a sitting-room with a dining area and acquire middle-class cultural habits.

The architects also introduced aesthetic embellishments in the houses based on the notion that an aesthetic domestic environment would spiritually enrich the farm labourer. Rietveld and his son Jan (1919-1986) devised facades in various colours, for example red, yellow and blue, and added coloured wire-glass features. J. Niegeman (1902-1977) and the landscape architect M. Ruys (1904-1999) offered to design a model house and model garden, so that the agricultural workers might learn how to furnish a modern house and garden both practically and aesthetically. Despite this aesthetic and modern solution, typical agricultural lifestyles also played a role in the design process. For example, all the houses were given a kitchen garden for the cultivation of vegetables. There were also discussions about constructing hen-houses and the provision of small fields for growing potatoes. The social geographer Hovens Greve was most insistent that the designers, as 'intellectual city-dwellers', had to learn about life in the polder via contacts with social organizations in the polder and the Bond van Plattelandsvrouwen ('Dutch Rural Women's Organization'). For example, he pointed out that, besides a shower on the upper bedroom floor, a shower with an ample changing room on the ground floor close to the back door was desirable, so that the agricultural worker could refresh himself as soon as he got home after a gruelling day working on the land. Hovens Greve also emphasized that the recreational activities of the farm worker would not be so intellectual in nature, but would instead involve rather simple handiwork. This included the keeping of chickens, pigeons and rabbits and the preserving of vegetables by the women. Facilities for this, such as a pantry for preserving-jars and livestock pens therefore ought to be present in and adjacent to the home.

Due to the rapid mechanization of agriculture, the demographics of Nagele have changed drastically since construction began. Agricultural workers no longer live there, and people of independent means and the retired have discovered the village. The influx of new residents and the progressive diminution of the size of households prompted an expansion to the south of the village with 124 houses, realized between 1982 and 1989, which thanks to the flat roofs and the organization around a green still respects the spirit of the original Nagele. Part of the woodland belt was cut down for construction of the neighbourhood. Despite this impact on the urban plan, the design of Nagele is an important design in 20th-century architectural history in both a national and international context. The original street layout is still intact; the houses, churches and schools are still standing. This is the reason why there are national as well as international initiatives to preserve Nagele as a monument of Nieuwe Bouwen architecture. Nagele enjoys protected status under Dutch law, and the Museum Nagele, where the impressive design history of Nagele is exhibited, has been housed in the former Catholic church for the last five years.

The international DOCOMOMO organization, an international working party for the documentation and conservation of modern architecture, recently included the village of Nagele on its register. This ratifies the place of the village of Nagele as part of our (inter)national modern architecture heritage.

1957-1964
Voorhof Delft

A.M. de Jonglaan
A.V. Scheltamaplein
A. Dekenlaan
A. van der Leeuwlaan
A. Roland Holstlaan
A. Verweylaan
A. Coolenlaan
B. Wolfflaan
Brederopad
Delflandplein
D. Costerplein
E. du Perronlaan
F. van Eedenlaan
G. Gezellelaan
H. Marsmanlaan
H. Gorterhof
I. Boudier-Bakkerstraat
I. da Costalaan
J.J. Potgieterlaan
J.J. Slauerhofflaan
J. van Lenneppad
J. Perklaan
J. Campertlaan
Kruithuisweg
L. van Deysselhof
L. Couperuslaan

M. Nijhofflaan
M. ter Braaklaan
Minervaweg
Multatuliweg
N. Beetslaan
Papsouwselaan
Provinciale Weg
Voorhofdreef
Vulcanusweg
Westlandseweg.
W. Bilderdijkhof
W. de Merodestraat
W. Kloospad

W. Wissing **Parcel allotment plan, Voorhof II, 1962**

NAI collection, Wissing archive

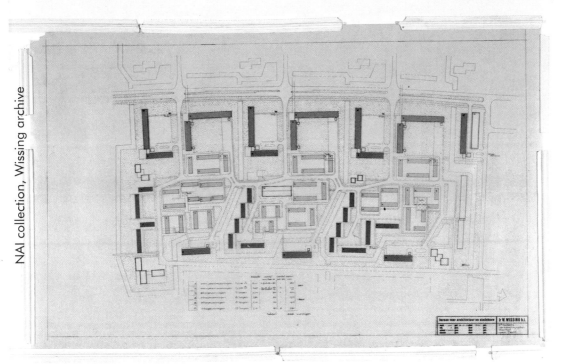

In the definitive plan, the number of dwellings was significantly increased.

Groosman architecture firm **Dwellings, circa 1964, floorplan**

NAI collection, Groosman archive

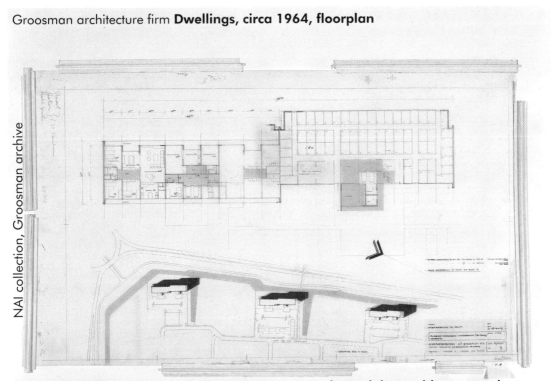

Although criticism of the high-rises grew, surveys showed that residents were happy with their dwellings. In this dwelling floorplan a grand piano has even been drawn in, emphasizing the generous proportions of the rooms.

J. Tol **Gallery-flat buildings, Voorhof, maquette**

NAI collection, Wissing archive

Maquette of a medium-rise and high-rise gallery-flat building by W. Wissing. At the ends of the buildings, the balconies wrap around the whole apartment.

. Wissing **Urban plan for Voorhof II, 1964, maquette**

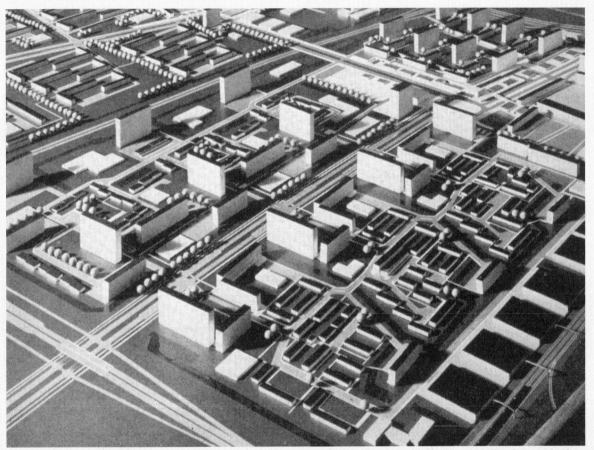

he Voorhofdreef, the traffic artery that links the district to the centre of Delft, runs right through the plan.
he clusters of gallery-flat buildings line this avenue like a buffer, with medium- and low-rise construction
ehind them.

Groosman architecture firm **Gallery-flat building, circa 1964, façade**

NAI collection, Groosman archive

This form of construction led to criticism in the 1970s from architects and urban planners in the Forum movement, namely that the human scale had been lost. They introduced the concepts of identity, cluster, place, shelter and integration. These were supposed to give expression to the characteristics of a environment, neighbourhood, district or city fit for human habitation.

projekt
PORTIEKBOUW TE DELFT.

gew   c
gew   b
get ♯ 17-11-'69   a

GEVEL OOSTZIJDE.

schaal 1:200

architektenbureau e.f. groosman n.v.
architekt medewerker a. koopmans d. sierig.

werk 67070

keerweer 1   rotterdam · 2   telefoon 010 · 13 47 95

tek. 8.

60/80

Voorhofdreef (1965 photo)

NAI collection, Wissing archive

The Voorhof has one of the highest residential densities in Europe – around 13,000 people live in a 10-hectare strip.

Voorhofdreef (photo circa 1972)

NAI collection, Stichting Wonen archive

The most ideal housing environment for children, according to S.J. van Embden, was the single-family dwelling. The post-war housing shortage and the population explosion, however, made construction in high densities necessary.

Voorhof (photo circa 1972)

NAI collection, Wissing archive

Building in the Voorhof became an assembly-line process, through the introduction of new construction systems such as prefabrication and on-site casting.

The Voorhof in Delft (1957-1964)
Joosje van Geest

The Voorhof in Delft, immediately south of the historic city centre, is characterized by a large number of high-rise flats. This residential development was realized in the 1960s and has one of the highest housing densities in Europe. There are about 13,000 people living in the Voorhof and there are varied shopping facilities and good transport connections, yet that high density is hardly noticeable thanks to the many tall trees, public gardens and parkland strips. In the 1950s and '60s, the post-war population explosion spawned unprecedented growth of the towns and cities in the western provinces of the Netherlands. The economy was booming, and the 'man in the street' was also carried on and up with this wave. The automobile became the ultimate symbol of social emancipation. The widespread availability of radio and television led to a process of mental urbanization. The countryside, already having to yield more and more of its agrarian functions, fell under the spell of the city for good. The baby boom coupled with social and economic progress led to spectacular prognoses and heated discussions about the future organization of our country, and the Randstad in particular. For example, in 1962, Statistics Netherlands predicted that the country's population would reach 20 million by the year 2000.

The architect and urban planner S.J. van Embden (1904-2000), who was closely involved with the development of the Poptahof (Voorhof I, 1957) as designer and adviser, made no secret of the fact that he considered the single-family dwelling and especially the detached house with garden to be the ideal family accommodation. However, like many of his contemporaries he also believed categorically that high-rise was the only way to prevent the anticipated densification and infill of the Randstad. The ideal scenario was to have a ring of cities in the western provinces of the Netherlands, each separated by four-kilometer buffer zones and set around the non-built-up 'Green Heart'. The Randstad cities would have to build in high densities to the outside of that ring. Moreover, the construction of flats would at last resolve the housing crisis in the low-price sector, which was still subject to acute shortages some 15 years after the Second World War. Thanks to developments in construction engineering, it was now profitable to build residential flats with low rents. Between the wars, this form of housing had still been unfeasible for working-class families because of the high construction costs.

In the early 1960s, a wave of high-rise swept across the Netherlands. The new functional residential areas consisted of various block types, such as low-rise housing, medium-rise walk-up flats and high-rise gallery-access flats, which were arranged in a repeating residential cluster or footprint. The Poptahof in Delft was one of the first and most attractive districts with high-rise. Arranged in eight residential clusters on either side of centrally positioned, tapering public gardens with water features, it is a sound and well-structured composition in which accommodates about 1,000 dwellings. An L-shaped perimeter of low-rise shops and taller commercial buildings links the development to the Delflandplein and the surrounding neighbourhoods.

Van Embden had originally proposed clusters with slender tower blocks of 12 storeys in combination with low-rise blocks of gallery-access flats and single-family dwellings. It was thus possible to achieve a high density while still creating an open distribution of building plots amidst plenty of green space. Unfortunately the tower blocks proved to be too expensive. The construction company proposed realizing inexpensive gallery-access flats using the MUWI system (a stacked concrete-block construction system for high-rise named after Muys & de Winter, the building contractors who devised it). Van Embden managed to integrate these blocks in the already realized street layout by removing a large proportion of the planned lower-rise gallery-access flats. This allowed a more generous spacing of the buildings in the neighbourhood and 10 per cent more housing units. In terms of the urban plan, however, this put pressure on the relationship between the residential neighbourhood and the shopping arcade. The distinct separation between housing and businesses was abandoned, and shops were accommodated on the ground floor of a residential block of flats, with parking nuisance as a result.

The basic idea for Voorhof II (1961) also used clusters with high-, medium- and low-rise blocks. A shopping centre and a high-rise block of flats for students were planned opposite the Poptahof. Initially the planners wanted to build high-rise blocks set at right angles on either side of the main road (Voorhofdreef), with blocks gradually decreasing in height in a U-shaped layout within a rectangular street plan. In the definitive plan by the urban planner W. Wissing, the total number of dwellings was increased substantially. The high-rise flats of 16 storeys along the Voorhofdreef were extended with lower wings of nine storeys and stand meandering along the main road. In this strip covering an area of more than 10 hectares the density is now no less than 122 dwellings per hectare. To the rear, in the central zone, there are low-rise blocks in a staggered sequence set along diagonal roads. The east side of the area is terminated by blocks of six storeys. Though the indented layout of the low-rise central area provides much greater variety, it still results in a lack of clarity. The significance of Voorhof II Oost rests much sooner in the intensive collaboration between clients, architects and contractors, which resulted in a revolutionary construction process of unprecedented efficiency for that time. With the introduction of new construction methods such as system building using prefabricated elements and on-site poured concrete construction, the Voorhof ushered in the era of the wholesale modernization of the construction industry, in which inexpensive, high-quality flats with lifts and central heating were built as if rolling off a conveyor belt.

In the mid-1970s, when the welfare state was in its prime, there was hard-hitting criticism of post-war planning. According to many, the repetitiveness of the blocks resulted in monotonous residential neighbourhoods. Although psychological studies indicated that flat residents were happy with their homes, the large-scale living environment was condemned as inhuman. 'High-rise neurosis' led to increasing suburbanization, with young families making an exodus from the city en masse for a terraced house in one of the growth cores in and around the Randstad. Dozens of the country's tower blocks had to contend with low occupancy rates, and because of the low rents they drew the socially disadvantaged and immigrants. The high turnover rate of tenants and associations with vandalism and dilapidation reinforced the negative image of the high-rise estates.

The usual social problems have now been signalled in the Poptahof in Delft as well, on top of which the dwellings are too small and of insufficient quality. Some of the dwellings are therefore to be renovated in the near future (the high-rise gallery-access flats), while others are to be demolished (the single-family housing and low-rise gallery-access flats). With the construction of new owner-occupied houses with ground access in the subsidized and free-market sectors, the goal is to increase the original number of houses by 30 per cent. With a more varied and bigger selection of housing, the planners hope to attract a more balanced population. The shopping centres along the development's periphery are also being tackled, so that the Poptahof will gain improved car-parking facilities and present a more clear-cut profile to the surrounding areas. The demolition of inexpensive flats (only 40 years old) and construction of low-rise housing for the owner-occupied market seem to be successful strategies which are being implemented in other residential areas from the 1950s and '60s.

1968-2004
Almere

Almere Haven

Centrum-Haven
De Gouwen
De Grienden
De Hoven
De Marken
De Meenten
De Velden
De Werven
De Wierden
Almere Hout
Overgooi

Almere Stad

Danswijk
Filmwijk
Kruidenwijk
Literatuurwijk
Muziekwijk
Noorderplassen
Parkwijk
Staatsliedenwijk
Stadscentrum

Stedenwijk
Tussen de Vaarten
Verzetswijk
Waterwijk

Almere Buiten

Bloemenbuurt
Bosrandpark
Bouwmeesterbuurt
Eilandenbuurt
Faunabuurt
Indische buurt
Landgoederenbuurt
Molenbuurt
Oostvaardersbuurt
Regenboogbuurt
Seizoenenbuurt

of various housing and green areas

NAI collection, Hosper archive

Landscape architect A. Hosper was one of the people in the Almere project bureau with a definite vision. His designs for the cohesion between city and landscape formed the foundation for the present-day greenbelt structure, a highly defining element of the city.

Rijksdienst IJsselmeerpolders/ Almere project bureau **Design for first phase of Almere Haven, 1974-1976, initial study**

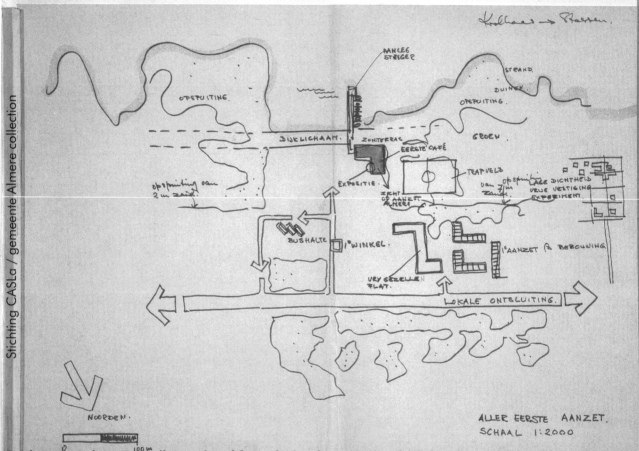

Designers such as T. Koolhaas aimed for a design for a city in which freedom and diversity in housing environments were key. The elements named in this sketch are partly representative of the later development of the city: bus lane, singles apartment block, low density and unrestricted location selection.

Van den Broek en Bakema **Centre of Almere Haven, 2nd and 3rd phase, 1976-1977, plan area maquette**

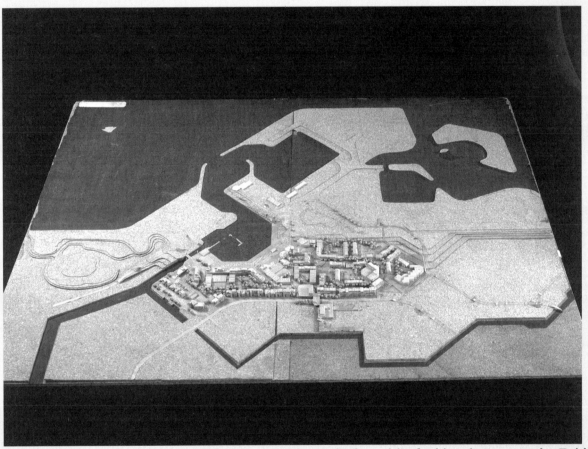

The urban planning and small-scale in-fill of Almere-Haven, in the spirit of a historic town on the Zuider-zee, marks a significant contrast to the emptiness of the reclaimed land of the Flevopolder. In the design, the buildings are grouped around the harbour and there is integration of employment, housing, and recreation.

Van den Broek en Bakema **Centre of Almere Haven, 2nd and 3rd phase, 1976-1977, impressions of various streetscapes**

... de haven, met een lage en een hoge kade ...

... en met ... wor...

... dan het plein bij de winkels, afdalend naar ...

... de smalle ... win...

ALMERE—HAVEN—centrum 2^e en 3^e fase
architectengemeenschap van den broek en bakema

NAI collection, Van den Broek en Bakema archive

A representative presentation sheet of Almere-Haven: a cozy town, with a harbour, lock, narrow shopping streets and a central role for public transport.

J. van Stigt **Schoolwerf dwellings, 1974-1976, aerial photo of first buildings in Almere Haven (photo circa 1976)**

Stichting CASLa / gemeente Almere collection

The first dwellings in Almere were designed by J. van Stigt. They are repetitive structures, typical of the 'New Amsterdam School', a group of A. van Eyck's students.

D. Apon / Apon Van den Berg Ter Braak Tromp Architekten **Dwellings, shops, offices in Almere Haven, 1975, view of façades along the Marktgracht (photo circa 1980)**

NAI collection, Bakema archive

The fact that the first buildings designed for the new Almere still looked rather traditional led to a great deal of criticism and incomprehension. At three to four dwelling levels, these buildings in the centre were initially the highest in Almere-Haven.

D. Apon / Apon Van den Berg Ter Braak Tromp Architekten **Dwellings, shops, offices in centre of Almere Haven, 1975, floorplans of 2-, 3-, 4-, 5- and 7-room dwellings**

NAI collection, Bakema archive

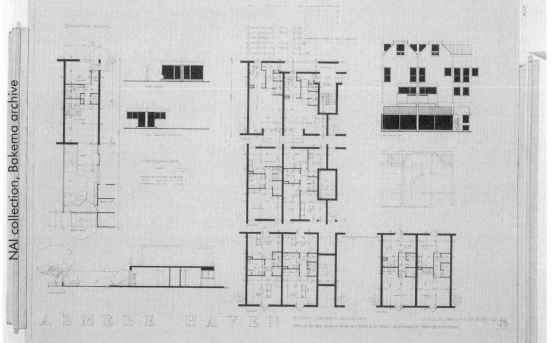

D. Apon, with these first dwellings in Almere Haven, fulfilled the wishes of the Almere project bureau to offer many different dwelling types.

J. de Groot / Van den Broek en Bakema **Embankment dwellings in Almere Haven, 1979-1980, view of tower blocks from the dike, in the direction of the centre of Almere Haven**

NAI collection, Van den Broek en Bakema archive

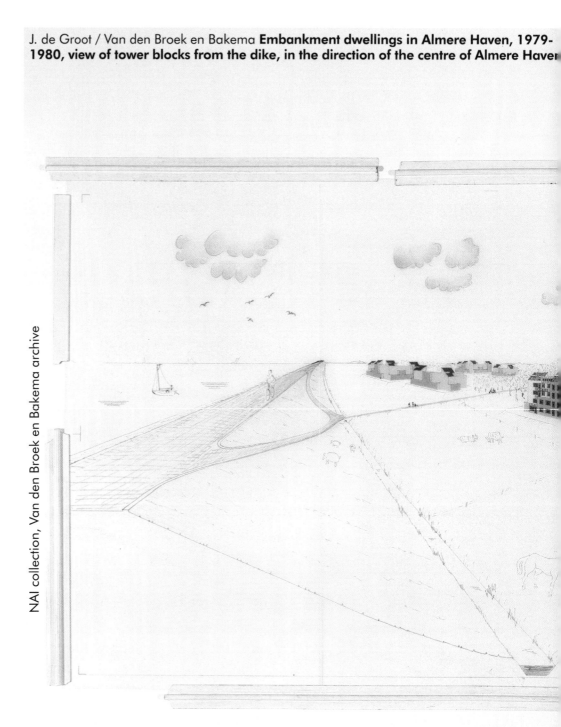

The firm of Van den Broek and Bakema, following the commission to produce a layout plan for the second and third phases of the centre of Almere Haven, came up with this design for embankment dwellings, directly behind the Gooimeer dike.

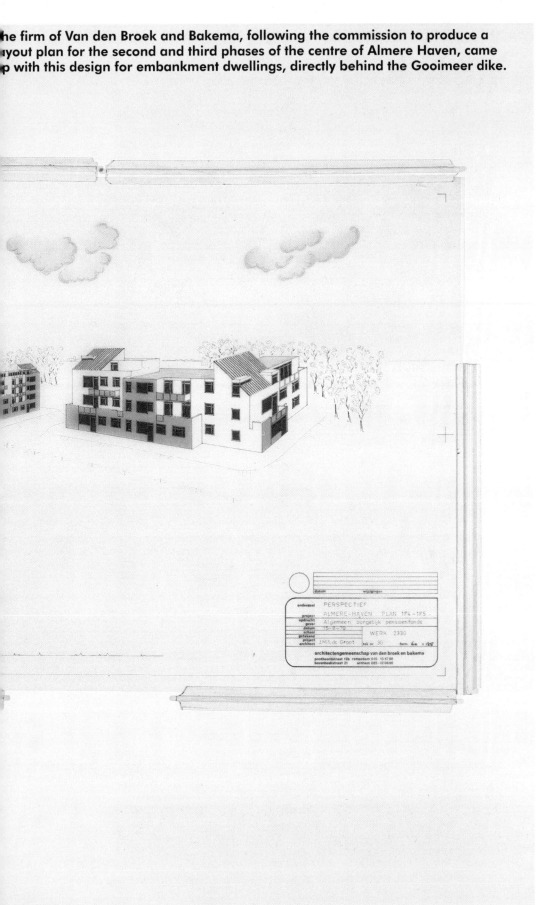

Various architects **De Realiteit, 1985-1986, view on some of the realised projects (photo circa 1987)**

Stichting CASLa / gemeente Almere collection

The designs in this neighbourhood come from the 'Temporary Housing' competition launched in 1985 by the foundation De Fantasie.

L. van der Pol / Atelier Zeinstra van der Pol **Rooie donders, Regenboogbuurt Almere Buiten, 1997-1998 (photo circa 1998)**

photograph by Rob 't Hart

The residential tower blocks illustrate how the low-rise town of Almere is slowly turning into a 'complete' city. The three 'rooie donders' ('red devils') quickly became treasured 'landmarks'.

F. Alkemade / Office for Metropolitan Architecture **Almere Stad city centre, 1994 (initial design), detail of maquette**

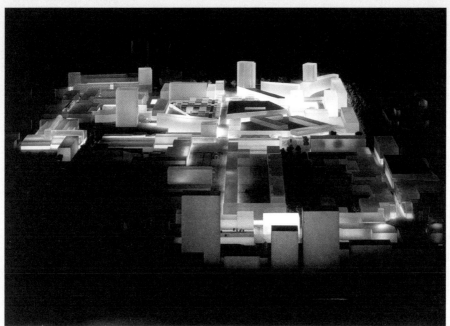

An important element in OMA's design is the curved surface under which traffic and parking functions are planned. On the upper level and in other sections will come a mixture of dwellings, shops, hotel, cinema and other entertainment functions.

F. Alkemade / Office for Metropolitan Architecture **Almere Stad city centre, 1994 (initial design), detail of maquette**

In his masterplan, R. Koolhaas blatantly set out to counter Almere's image: low-rise buildings, low densities and a grid system in Almere Stad. His masterplan is characterized by high-rises, high function density and a rejection of the existing grid.

Lifestyles in the polder
JaapJan Berg

Almere is the perfect translation of the ultimate Dutch suburban domestic ideal: living amidst greenery and yet close to all the urban conveniences. The influence of Ebenezer Howard's garden city concept as formulated around 1900 can be detected in almost all 20th-century expansion plans. After the Second World War, the 'neighbourhood principle' brought about a definitive decentralization of the city. However, it was only when the first complete new cities were designed for the new Flevopolder – Lelystad starting from 1959, and Almere from 1968 – and when greater prosperity made suburbia accessible for everyone that the implications of this ideal could be fully explored.

Yet Almere is not shaped exclusively by the familiar garden city model. The success of the existing city is primarily the result of the efforts to devise a flexible urban design within which it is possible to react to changes and developments. The design has proven that the tempestuous growth of a new city should not be trammelled by a rigid masterplan. A flexible and phased organization affords sufficient anchoring, direction and cohesion. In the rapidly expanding city of today, the validity and success of that ambition is still evident in the tracts of fallow land with temporary vegetation which are reserved for later use. Partly owing to that pre-planned dynamism and flexibility, Almere has been able to evolve into the leading laboratory for Dutch domestic architecture of the last 25 years.

The city has an architectural tradition that is to a large degree focused on creativity and individuality – albeit in diverse formal conventions, from 'little farmsteads' to 'architects' architecture' in experimental little neighbourhoods. To a large degree these architectural qualities now determine the image and branding of this city and are most evident in a selection of realized neighbourhoods – partly open-air exhibitions for domestic architecture – which run like a leitmotiv through the recent history of the city: de Fantasie (1982), de Realiteit (1986), Muziekwijk (NWR BouwRai, 1990), Filmwijk (NWR BouwRai, 1992), Regenboogbuurt (1997), Eilandenbuurt (Gewild Wonen, 2001) and the Stadshart (the 'City Heart', from 1994).

Almere lies in Zuidelijk Flevoland (the southern section of the youthful province of Flevoland, on reclaimed land) and is the first polder which was programmed as a component of the Randstad's infrastructure rather than as a productive agricultural landscape. \In 1958, the persistent housing shortage, the lack of space in the Randstad and the need for new rail- and roadways from the Randstad to the east and north of the country were given as the most important arguments for land reclamation. Almere's designers have in many respects learnt lessons from the plans made by C. van Eesteren in 1959 for the Rijksdienst IJsselmeerpolders (RIJP, the government body for the IJsselmeer polders). Lelystad was based on the notion of functionalist urbanism, with a strict separation of functions and a mono-functional approach to the residential environment. The design of Lelystad was characterized by a big-city traffic structure, which stood in the way of an innovative, more informal and flexible approach to the city.

Both in the design vision and the actual design of the first core, Almere Haven, the reaction to and lessons learnt from Lelystad are clearly visible. Whereas Lelystad was a product of the no-nonsense approach of the post-war decades, Almere Haven, with its inward-looking courtyard structure and the extensively debated planning process, is a typical product of the 1970s. A number of aspects have been re-applied nonetheless, for example the separate traffic flows for motorized traffic, public transport and cyclists. The origins of the urban plan for Almere are therefore, in various respects, rooted in Lelystad. The more comprehensive and thorough preparation of the plans here has proven to be a big advantage for Almere. In addition, the prospective location has, over the course of time, proven to be more strategic and the city has been able to profit more from the influx of new inhabitants and a greater potential for economic growth. Perhaps still most important, however, is that in Almere the freedom of choice for the critical housing consumer was crucial from the very first plans, and was also used as an argument to attract people to establish their homes there. The first residents were mainly from the Randstad, where there was a lack of suitable accommodation thanks to urban renewal. Being relatively close by, Almere did its best to offer a much higher level of residential comfort and a palette of choices. In addition, the greater prosperity of the 1960s brought the terraced house in a green setting within financial reach for many. More and more people exchanged the city, where high-rise and multi-storey construction prevailed, for the countryside.

Crucial for the success of Almere was the now legendary Project-bureau Almere, which was largely staffed by enthusiastic young professionals, many of them academics, from a range of disciplines. D. Frieling, T. Koolhaas, H. van Willigen, W. Segeren and P. Davelaar were among the trendsetting designers and planners who worked there. This idealistic group often failed to strike the right note with the more agricultural tradition of the RIJP staff and – completely in keeping with the mood of the 1970s – they took plenty of time to consider and discuss the many options and versions of the plans. Projectbureau Almere designed the framework of a poly-nuclear city that was projected to initially house between 100,000 and 250,000 inhabitants.

Initially three cores were planned, each with a specific living environment determined by the locale: Almere Haven on the Gooimeer lake, Almere Stad alongside the central lake that was created later on – the Weerwater – and Almere Buiten in the middle of the polder, hemmed in by the later routes of the railway and the A6 highway. With low-rise initially representing more than 90 per cent of construction, and with the proximity of greenery and urban conveniences, Almere became a successful model for the amalgamation of urban and rural into a new urban domestic landscape. The value that these designers – especially landscape architect A. Hosper – attached to the proximity of greenery and landscape is clearly evident from the high priority of the planting of greenery in the still-empty polder. 'Green City Almere' was in effect planted first and built later. The first substantial planting, alongside the future A6 motorway, was symbolically named the 'Beginbos' ('First Forest'). Characteristic of the drive and confidence of the designers in the Almere project was that they initially also sketched and designed for future cores like Pampus, Hout and Poort.

Almere's poly-nuclear organization was not only informed by the lessons learnt with Lelystad, but also by the condition of the land in this part of the polder and the goal of flexibility. The neighbouring Gooi region, a highly desirable residential area, is often cited as an example: a green yet (sub)urbanized residential area with a central core and a number of sub-cores, each with its own character and identity, each subdivided by green zones. This principle of autonomous living environments per nucleus was refined in the further development of Almere into the specific design of neighbourhoods. The main objective was to provide a pleasant living environment of low-rise housing surrounded by greenery which could compete with the cities on the 'old' land. Due to the great flexibility of the plan, the different cores could grow independently of each other, and in their own way. That target flexibility was all the more necessary because there was initially a lack of clarity about the function and status of Almere. Should it become an independent core or an overflow area for Amsterdam or Utrecht, a metropolis or a dormitory? With the eventual decision taken by Frieling (as chief of the Projectbureau) to set the capacity of the first core at about 20,000 residents, it was already evident that this core had no chance of an autonomous existence. Thus the development of the two other cores was in fact a foregone conclusion. Finally, a technical issue, the unsuitability for construction of some of the subsoil in this part of the polder, formed an often-forgotten reason for the poly-nuclear layout.

Towards the end of the 1960s, the provinces of North Holland, Utrecht and Gelderland battled about the precise position of the first core, Almere Haven. The eventual decision was to build a central core of 130,000 residents, the later Almere Stad, and six surrounding sub-cores of 20,000 residents each. That was the maximum size which, following the vision of the neighbourhood principle, permitted a direct identification with the living environment. Almere Haven's location was clearly the result of a compromise, because it lies more or less in the middle of the prospective bank-to-bank connections with the provinces of North Holland and Utrecht. In the further planning for Almere Haven, the goal is a varied urban living environment. Instead of an all-embracing urban plan that risks monotony, only a global structure was set out, the 'vlekkenplan', with vague 'splotches' indicating the outline of prospective development areas to be filled in by different architects later. The various concentric circles remain clearly visible on many drawings, even once the shape and size of the neighbourhoods has been decided in greater detail.

The dominant figures within Projectbureau Almere were, moreover, not the actual designers, but representatives of the 'soft' sector, namely sociologists, social geographers and planners. Under their influence, it was the psychological experience of the living environment – the 'living milieu' – that took centre stage, rather than functional aspects. With its 'living beside the water', the Almere Haven core was given a distinctive atmosphere, alluding to the traditional coastal towns on the Zuiderzee. This was underscored by the canals along which the houses were built, twentieth-century canalside properties in traditional brick architecture. To many critics it was incomprehensible that a completely new city should be shaped in such a quasi-traditional manner. Accusations of petty-mindedness and holding bourgeois values high also hung in the air. The functions of home, work and recreation were not separated but in fact integrated as far as possible. Motorized traffic was kept out of town as far as possible in favour of public transport, while the small-scale structure of the urban plan and its many pedestrian zones was determined by 'walkability' from the stops for public transport. By funnelling the surrounding green structure, the polder landscape, into the city via green wedges, the concept of living in green surroundings was reinforced. The design of Almere Haven therefore marked a break, in various respects, with the heritage of modernism and the Congrès Internationaux d'Architecture Moderne (CIAM). The organic urbanism of designers joined together in Team X was the inspiration for the 'cauliflower urbanism' or 'Barbapapa urbanism' that was presented as an alternative.

The first phase of Almere Haven was elaborated by three architects. J. van Stigt and A. Mastenbroek designed the first residential neighbourhoods and D. Apon designed the first structures in the centre. Other architects contributed designs for the core later on, for example Van den Broek en Bakema, H. Hertzberger and also C. Dam, while R. Koolhaas/OMA designed his first building to be realized in the Netherlands here, a police station. All the architects involved designed a complete living milieu within the brief stipulated by the Projectbureau, which was elaborated down to the smallest details such as garden fences and paving.

The Projectbureau even put together catalogues with the title 'Programmering van Woongebieden' ('Programming of Residential Areas'), which provided typologies and guidelines for the envisaged variety. Despite the ambition to take into account the wishes of the residents, of which there was hardly any insight during the first phase, within the profession this populism was condemned as 'new narrow-mindedness'. However, this pursuit of variety and flexibility, coupled with the combination of architectural ambition and an average annual production of about 3,000 houses, laid a fundamental basis for the development of Almere as an important laboratory for Dutch domestic architecture during the last 25 years. When work began on the intended main nucleus, Almere Stad, around 1978 – fairly soon after the commencement of construction work on Almere Haven – the approach, in the same vein as the first core, was adapted to the latest insights in the fields of architecture and urban planning as well as demographic developments in the Netherlands. This capacity to adapt would manifest itself on a number of other occasions in the course of recent history. Since the ambition and housing production were founded on a well-oiled collaboration of civil servants (initially at state level, later at a municipal level), designers and building contractors, Almere could be designed at the cutting-edge of developments. The youthful Almere thus grew into an independent city with its own big-city amenities where established and younger designers were regularly given the chance to show off their abilities.

At the same time, Almere developed into a place where individual personal housing preferences were honoured to varying degrees. The first step in a subsequent series of key housing projects in Almere was the neighbourhood 'de Fantasie' on the Weerwater lake. In the early 1980s, a number of special designs were realized there, selected from entries for a competition with the title 'Ongewoon Wonen' – 'Unusual Living'. The competition was organized by the 'de Fantasie' foundation, and the plots of land were a gift from the Rijksdienst IJsselmeerpolders to the future Municipality of Almere. Designers such as J. Benthem, P. Loerakker and, at a later stage, R. van Zuuk designed high-quality and eccentric houses for themselves. The little neighbourhood soon enjoyed (inter)national attention, and was a first concretization of having an influence over one's own living environment, as promoted by the Projectbureau. For Almere, the result and the response were an eye-opener, and were quickly picked up by the market players in the construction sector.

This seminal initiative was followed in 1986 by a similar neighbourhood on the banks of the Noorderplassen lakes, 'de Realiteit'. This also involved designs for and by designers, such as T. Koolhaas, Holvast en Van Woerden, E. Böhtlingk and others. After this, the market took over the baton from the architects, and in the 1990s there were two open-air exhibitions in new neighbourhoods in Almere Stad in quick succession, both organized in association with NWR BouwRAI. The first exhibition took place in 1990 in the 'Muziekwijk' ('Music District'), appropriately enough it was also the first neighbourhood to be wholly developed by the youthful Municipality of Almere. The model neighbourhood provides an overview of the current possibilities in new forms of living. A select group of architects left their visiting cards there. Remarkable designs included the 'Woonwerkhuizen' – 'Live-Work Houses' – by Hertzberger and the 'Meerfasenwoningen' – 'Multiphase Houses' – by Koolhaas. The success of this first exhibition led to a second one as soon as 1992, this time in the Filmwijk ('Film District') of Almere Stad. On this occasion the starting-point was to show the novel ideas for the 'building of tomorrow'. The great diversity of submissions included designs by the Netherlands' most famous architects at that time: A. van Eyck, T. Bosch, S. Soeters, W. Quist and many others. After the development of the 'Regenboogbuurt' ('Rainbow District') in Almere Buiten (1997), where architects were given the brief to design within a compelling colour plan, there was a third outdoor exhibition in 2001, 'GeWild Wonen' ('Sought-After Housing'), which was organized by the Municipality of Almere itself, to celebrate the city's 25th anniversary.

At this location in Almere Buiten, now called Eilandenbuurt ('Islands Neighbourhood'), a spirited attempt was made to give concrete form to the discussion sparked by C. Weeber about a greater say for the housing consumer about his or her home, otherwise straitjacketed by a 'state-planned' housing market and over-regulation, which became known as 'Wilde Wonen' – 'Anarchistic Living'. Buyers and tenants of about 600 homes were to a greater or lesser degree given the chance to put together their own home, with the aid of construction kits or modular programmes devised by architects. Though the range of possibilities for the residents was still determined by the architect and developer, this neighbourhood was a logical consequence of a development in Almere which had begun with the designers of the Projectbureau and their plans for freedom of choice and specific living 'milieus' and had culminated in a neighbourhood where the residents were truly given a say. A building in the centre of Almere Buiten, the 'Doemere' do-it-yourself centre (1988) by Bakker en Verhoef is probably the ultimate symbol of a city where living, residents and the influence of lifestyles are pivotal.

The circle would seem complete, were it not for Almere now facing the even greater challenge of evolving further, into a full-fledged city with a projected population of 300,000. The strength of Almere is that it has consistently succeeded in incorporating these and other developments in an urban fabric based on the poly-nuclear structure – a concept which, with the densification of many open spaces between the cores, has now been semi-officially abandoned. It is this brilliant and infinitely flexible commingling of town and country that some people believe makes Almere the most modern city in the world.

The flexible form of Almere thus reflects a plethora of the urban planning and architectural trends of recent decades. And it continues to do that, because 'Los Almeres' is an ongoing adventure with a still uncertain outcome. The increasing individualization of living environments, increasingly determined by lifestyling, makes the flexible Almere model more relevant than ever. The definitive emancipation of Almere into a full-fledged city is now being executed in the centre of Almere Stad, as it undergoes trans-formation into a metropolitan megastructure to a masterplan by OMA. In Almere the city is continuously being reinvented.

1970-1986
Nieuwmarkt quarter Amsterdam

Keizersstraat
Koningsstraat
Korte Dijkstraat
Lastageweg
Nieuwe Hoogstraat
Nieuwe Jonkestraat
Nieuwe Ridderstraat
Recht Boomssloot
Sint Anthoniebreestraat
Zandstraat

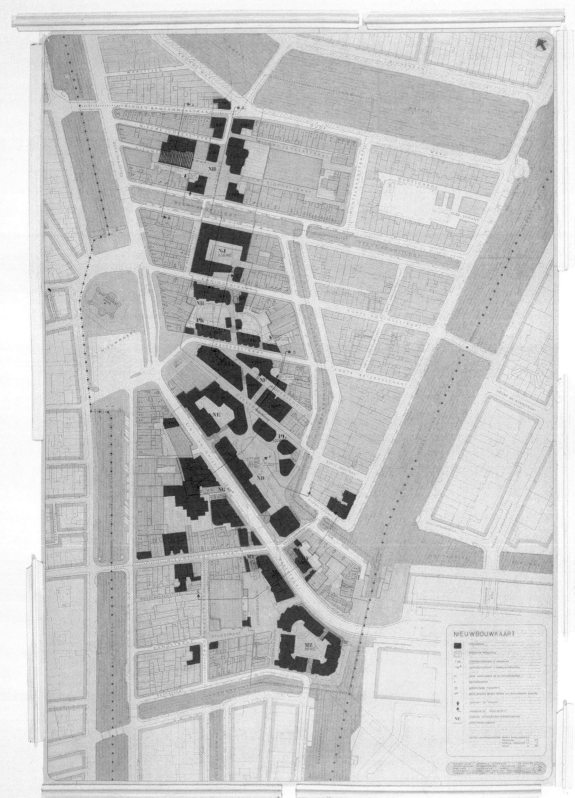

The new-build construction in the Nieuwmarkt quarter is indicated in dark red; the pink indicates the existing – or rather spared – buildings.

Th. Bosch **Pentagon housing complex, Sint Anthoniebreestraat, 1975-1983, floorplan**

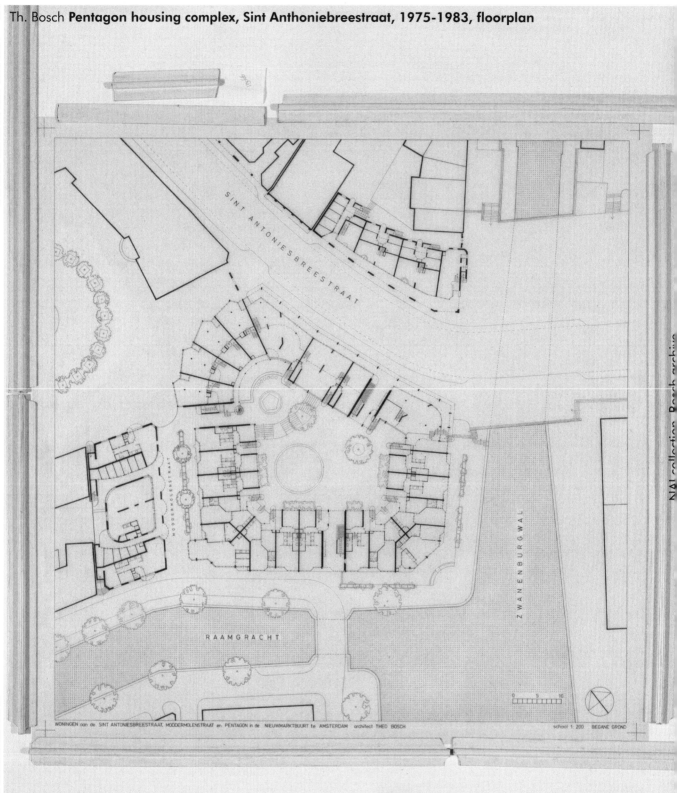

The ground floor of the Pentagon (1975-1983) by architect Th. Bosch. The block contains 87 porch-access dwellings, shops, studios and dwellings for the elderly.

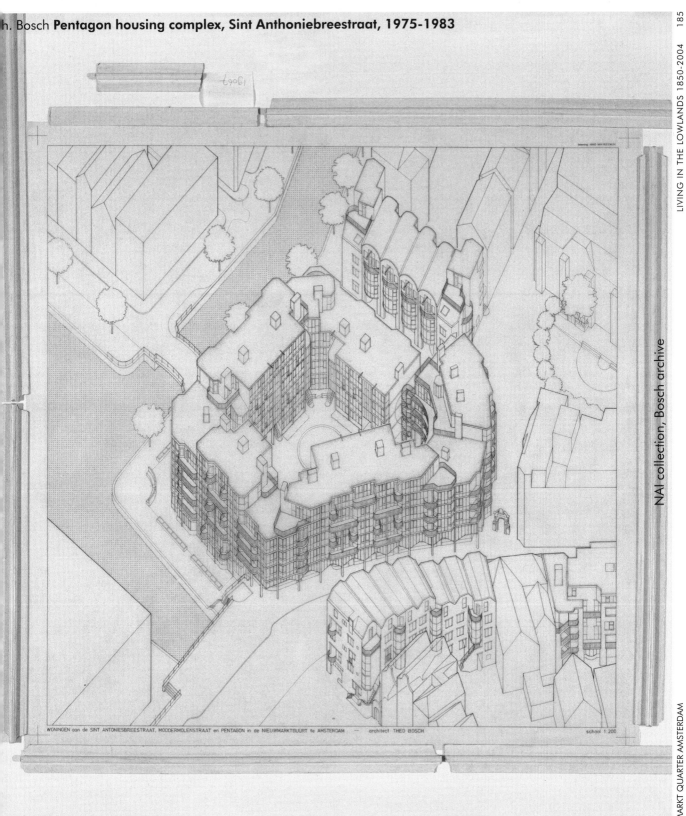

NAI collection, Bosch archive

WONINGEN aan de SINT ANTONIESBREESTRAAT, MOODERMOLENSTRAAT en PENTAGON in de NIEUWMARKTBUURT te AMSTERDAM — architect THEO BOSCH — schaal 1:200

Bird's-eye view of the Pentagon (the five-angled structure) on the Sint Antoniebreestraat. All dwellings have grand views. On this, architect Th. Bosch says, 'the idea is to give even a flat that is not a corner flat that quality.'

A. van Eyck, Th. Bosch, G. Knemeijer, P. De Ley en D. Tuijnman **Nieuwmarkt quarter, 1970, basic design principles for revitalization of Nieuwmarkt quarter**

NAI collection, Bosch archive

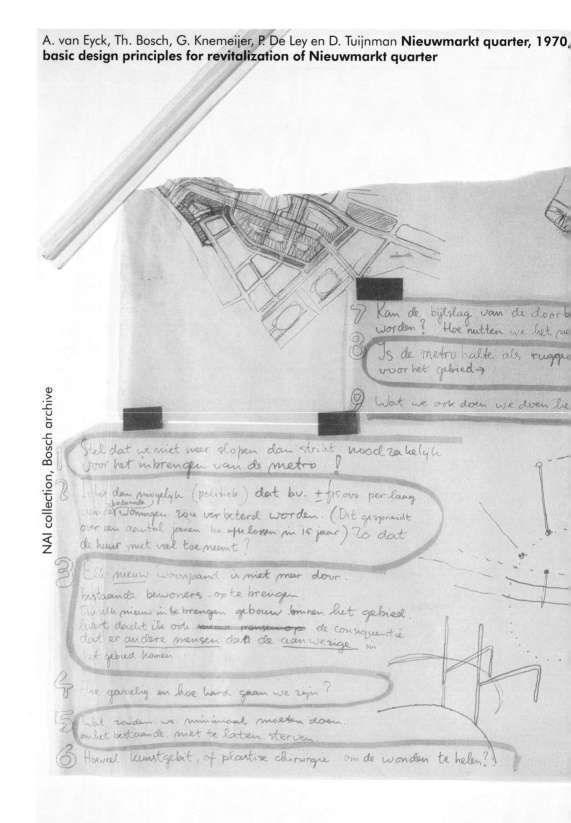

van Eyck's and Th. Bosch's basic premises for the revitalization of the Nieuwmarkt Quarter. Both architects were also concerned with such urban renewal principles as 'building for the community', good housing space with low housing costs and the preservation of social structures.

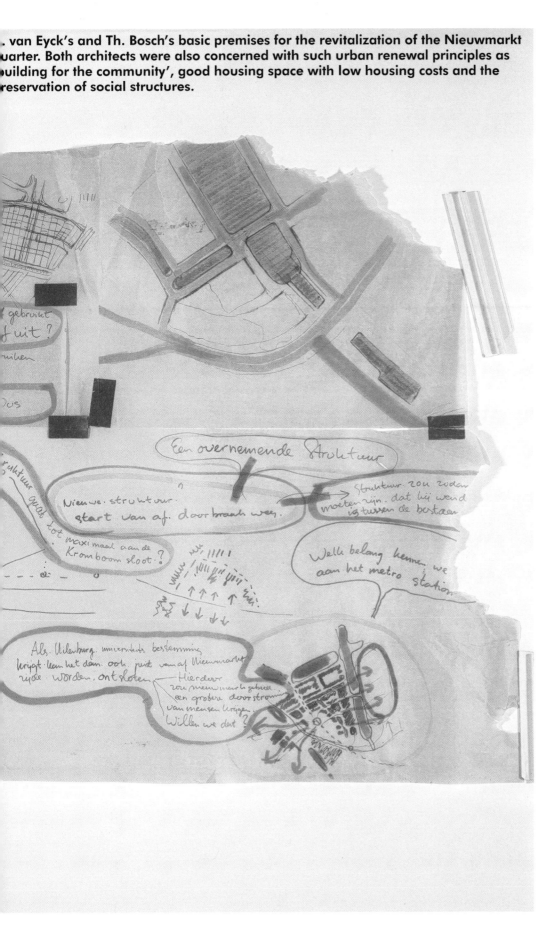

Nieuwmarkt quarter (1980 aerial photo)

Dienst Wonen collection, Amsterdam

Demolition for the metro's trajectory meanders like a snake through the Nieuwmarkt quarter. At bottom right the razing of the Waterlooplein for the construction of the Stopera (1980).

Nieuwmarkt quarter (1975 photo)

Dienst Wonen collection, Amsterdam

In 1975, the former Jewish quarter was a dilapidated area. The Nieuwmarkt quarter had been neglected for decades because redevelopment had to wait for large-scale city plans.

H. Borkent **New-build housing, Sint Antoniebreestraat, 1975-1983**

Dienst Wonen collection, Amsterdam

The two landmark residential houses in the middle of the block were saved from demolition at the last minute and had to be incorporated into the plan. They were suspended from the new construction, because their foundations were too poor.

Living in the Nieuwmarkt neighbourhood
Marcel Theunissen

The architecture bureau next to the lingerie shop, the antiquarian bookshop next to the sushi bar, houses old and new above and alongside: the varied cityscape and the intermingling of functions as well as public make the Nieuwmarkt neighbourhood one of the most colourful and vibrant residential areas in Amsterdam's city centre. These days, anyone who repeats the mantra that housing is everyone's right would soon be classified as an immature old dreamer, an anachronistic idealist, but views of this kind were repeatedly daubed on walls and hoardings in the days of defiance when the struggle for the preservation of the Nieuwmarkt neigh-bourhood as a residential area with small-scale business activity was at its most tempestuous. The Nieuwmarkt neighbourhood was the first urban regeneration project of any considerable size in the Netherlands. Even more important was the change in the attitude of government bodies towards historic city centres. In the Nieuwmarkt neighbourhood, though the battle about the metro was lost, the preservation of the intricate structure and mix of functions had considerably more weight as a moral victory.

Amsterdam's oldest port neighbourhood, which had been contributing to the city's economy since the 16th century, therefore deserved a better fate than ruthless razing. The pauperization as a result of industrialization had failed to prompt redevelopment and the neighbourhood, populated by migrants since days of yore, was on its last legs by the end of the Second World War.

The Nieuwmarkt neighbourhood was pretty much a dilapidated ghetto. The city council thought the area was ideally suited for the 'city-making' which had become fashionable after the war. The municipal Reconstruction Plan of 1953 was therefore also first and foremost a demolition plan. Housing would have to make way for an office district, cut through by a four-lane urban highway. The plan foundered a flood of resistance, but was given a new lease of life in 1962 with the resolution to build a metro line beneath the trajectory of the planned road artery. When this was approved by the city council in 1968, militant local residents and action groups brought a halt to the demolition of housing which was already underway. To resolve this deadlock, the city council decided to issue a competition in order to harmonize the municipal ambitions and, to a certain degree, the wishes of neighbourhood residents within the framework of the plan from 1953, which was still legally binding. Of the three revision plans submitted, in that respect the plan by the bureau of Aldo van Eyck (1918-1999) offered the best starting-points for discussion. Van Eyck and his colleagues grudgingly agreed to cooperate on the renewal of the neighbourhood. As it became obvious that the bureau was set on a new approach under the slogan 'the city heart as donor', Van Eyck and his new partner, Theo Bosch (1940-1994), won the confidence of the neighbourhood and all manner of interest groups. The urban highway was voted down by the city council, but the construction of the metro seemed inevitable. Van Eyck retreated into the background and most of the work fell on the shoulders of Bosch, who in 1974 was appointed as the coordinating architect for the reconstruction phase.

However, the promised rapid reconstruction failed to materialize. After a battle with the riot police in the sultry summer of 1975, the last properties on the Lastage – the neighbourhood's main artery –

were demolished, the only activity for the time being was feverish work on the metro. For a long time the neighbourhood continued to be a Mecca for speculators, who sent in the heavy-handed lads if there were squatted properties that had to be cleared, and it was nothing unusual that they could count on police support as well. As a counter-offensive, the housing bureau De Kraker ('The Squatter') was set up. Though the highway was officially shelved, there were still hardened, technocratic municipal planners who attempted to give the profile of a wide traffic artery to the allotted Sint Antoniebreestraat. Theo Bosch managed to thwart this, even though the street profiles, buildings lines and zoning scheme were not 'secured' until 1980, when the land-use plan drawn up by Bosch was approved.

In the meantime, new houses had been built in dribs and drabs, but Bosch's plan sealed the definitive prostration of the city council: the fine-meshed structure of the neighbourhood would remain intact and a few informal routes devised by Bosch were interwoven with it. The clear-cutting that had taken place for the sake of metro construction was remedied as best as possible by building on top of the metro tunnel. This expensive construction operation was made possible thanks to additional funding from the Stadsvernieuwings-fonds ('City Redevelopment Fund'). Bosch realized nine housing projects himself and supervised the work of Heuperman, Visser, Hagenbeek, Van Overbeek, Borkent, CAV, Van Rhijn, Tuynman, Nust, De Ley, Kolkman and De Haan.

Bosch also played a catalytic role in the public consultation process on urban redevelopment, which entailed working with design teams in which residents also had a say. He refused to be intimi-dated by the bureaucratic machinations and proved his case at the Grondbedrijf (Land Development Agency) when it turned out that the combination of housing with business space in the street-level substructure was beneficial to the economic and social functioning of the neighbourhood. Bosch also refused to be blinkered by 'Prescriptions and Hints' or legislation pertaining to social-sector housing in the Netherlands. He ensured a broadly differentiated spectrum of housing as well as variation in dwelling types, such as maisonettes and live/work spaces for artists.

The residents returned and since then have lived there better than ever. Bosch and the other architects enriched the housing with loggias, balconies, roof terraces and, in some cases, even light wells. While the first infill projects were realized in sturdy brick-built architecture, the use of colour and materials became increasingly varied during the reconstruction phase. Due to the high-density construction, at certain points the cityscape is somewhat cacophonic, and even Bosch thought it 'could have been toned down a touch', but the most important thing is that the neighbourhood is buzzing again.

Bosch's biggest personal contribution was the Pentagon residential complex (1975-1983). The shape of this pentagonal block was derived from the existing building lines and indentations, but the rich plasticity of the facades sprang first and foremost from the housing design. Light, the view and spaciousness were the guiding principles here. With one foot firmly on the metro tunnel, the complex stands like a beacon right where the car traffic should have torn into the neighbourhood. The Pentagon has a 'distinctive but smiling face', as Th. Bosch put it. It is a manifesto from the era when the historic city was rehabilitated as a place to live.

1984-1992
Prinsenland Rotterdam

A. Noorlandersingel
C. Kraanstraat
C. Kouwenbergzoom
D. Outerstraat
G. Breurstraat
G. Henningstraat
G. Terlouwstraat
G. Wagemansstraat
J. Mulsteestraat
J. Dutilhweg
K. Bothstraat
K. Dullemondstraat
M. Batenburgplein
M. Weezenaarstraat
M. Wesselingstraat
N. Griffijnstraat
P. van Rijsselstraat
P. Klapwijkstraat
Prins Alexanderlaan
Ringvaartplas
Ringvaartplasbuurt Oost

F. Palmboom, E. Bet and W. van Proosdij **Masterplan for Prinsenland, 1984, historical situation**

Structuurschets Prinsenland, 1984

Prinsenland, because of the peat that was produced here for centuries, was a great water area. Between 1850 and 1870 it was drained and parcelled out in rectangular plots. The ditches served to assure drainage in the marshy area.

F. Palmboom, E. Bet and W. van Proosdij **Masterplan for Prinsenland, 1984**

Structuurschets Prinsenland, 1984

In the 1984 Structural Plan, the traditional structure and buildings of the three ribbons, Kralingse Weg, Ringvaartweg en 's Gravenweg, were retained. With the Ringvaartplas lake, water has been reintroduced as an element.

Mecanoo Architecten **Urban plan, circa 1988**

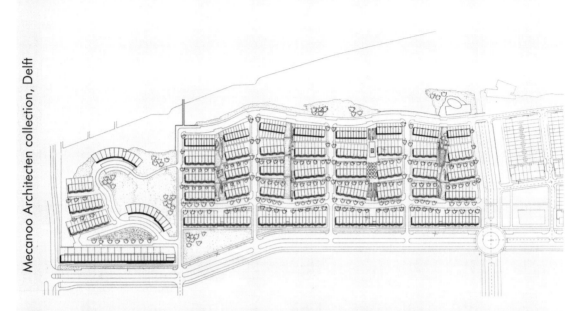

Mecanoo Architecten collection, Delft

Mecanoo not only designed the urban plan but also the dwellings and the housing environment. They wanted to realize an urban garden city, in which public and private greenbelts would reinforce the friendly, leafy atmosphere. The four theme gardens link the residential paths to one another.

Mecanoo Architecten **Residential-path dwellings, design 1989, completion 1991-1992, façades**

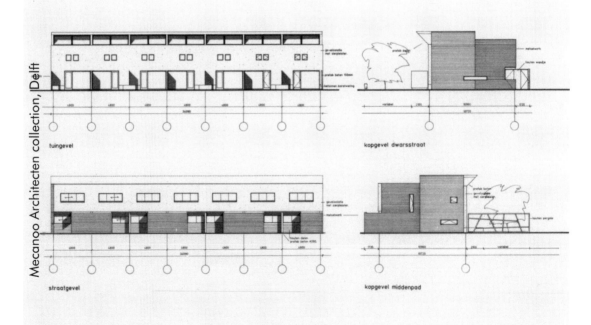

Mecanoo Architecten collection, Delft

tuingevel

kopgevel dwarsstraat

straatgevel

kopgevel middenpad

Façade views of the residential-path dwellings. The major portion of the 1,400 dwellings in the Ringvaartplas area consists of single-family dwellings of two storeys with a garden.

eneral view of Ringvaartplas area, 1988-1992 (photo circa 1995)

n the right the Schip residential building, in the centre three rows of dwellings. The two half-moon-
naped buildings are situated in the public greenbelt. Behind this the dwellings along the residential paths,
ordered on the right by stacked buildings in three levels, and on the left by the lakeside dwellings.

Mecanoo Architecten **'t Schip residential building, 1989-1992**

Maquette of the 't Schip residential building, with diverse dwelling types. The building varies in height from four to six levels.

Mecanoo Architecten **Japanese garden, 1989-1992, collage**

Mecanoo Architecten collection, Delft

Each of the four central green areas has its own theme. This is a collage of a Japanese garden, laid out with such Eastern symbols as azaleas, boulders and gravel representing water.

Mecanoo Architecten **English garden, 1989-1992 (photo circa 1995)**

photograph by Christian Richters

One of the central English-style gardens. The fences of the adjacent dwellings were prescribed. To reinforce the leafy character of the garden city, thick walls and high fences are not permitted in this area.

Mecanoo Architecten **Residential-path dwellings, 1989-1992, side façade (photo circa 1995)**

photograph by Christian Richters

Side façade of a residential-path dwelling. Each of the residential paths has its own character because each path is planted with different sorts of greenery.

From edge city to urban countryside
Aaron Betsky

In 1984, the office of landscape architect and urban planner Riek Bakker produced a plan for the development of an area of three square kilometers of agricultural land just to the east of the city of Rotterdam. In this ambitious 'Structure Outline Prinsenland' they called for a new approach to urban design: based on the existing landscape, but not afraid to make large gestures, it proposed a coherent vision of urbanity deeply rooted in place. As such, it became a model for many other residential developments in subsequent years. In one area, Ringvaart Plasbuurt Oost, the architecture firm Mecanoo created a concrete realization of this vision.

The plan, further developed by urban designer Fritz Palmboom, was based on his analysis of the site's geography and geometry. While the whole area had been a polder and agricultural land, Prinsenland's southern half consisted of thin, long meadows arranged in fan shapes, tied together along narrow, undulating streets of farmhouses that formed the old connector routes between east and west. The site's northern part was a larger-scaled grid of meadows without a clear focal element. Palmboom proposed leaving these grids as the organizing elements for the new neighborhoods. The southern section would be made up of a series of 'rooms' opening to the preserved agricultural axis and dotted with new housing elements. The northern section would have space for larger flat buildings and rowhouses, grouped around preserved open space in the form of parks and a cemetery. Connecting these two halves, bridging a height difference along the north-south axis of three meters, and strengthening the sense of the site as a connection between the city to the west and the park areas to the east, would be a curved lake. Along this monumental open space, that also celebrated the importance of water and its storage in one of the lowest parts of the Netherlands (up to eight metres below sea level), a new road would form an access spine along which the major shopping areas and facilities could be located.

Ringvaart Plasbuurt Oost was one of the last pieces to fulfil the vision of this plan, and the one that most fully realized the ambitions of Prinsenland's design at every scale. Designed by Mecanoo in 1988 and finished in 1992, it came in a period in which the firm was developing a way of fragmenting and recomposing the then standard, mass-produced forms of housing to create recognizable images and even monumental presence. Refusing to believe in the making of image over anonymous form, but also not interested in producing system-based structures that would express only processes of design and construction, Mecanoo made their buildings into domestic fragments of a newly revitalized and appreciated modern metropolis, often exported from the city centre into urban expansion areas.

In this case, the development consists of 545 housing units of mainly social housing. Over 300 of the units were single-family residences that Mecanoo arranged in four rows of four bars each, situated between the northeastern edge of the lake and the new access road. Two crescent-shaped blocks contain three-room apartments in a more park-like, open setting. Three additional bar-buildings then continue the main grid to the edge of the project's boundaries, where the tram line from Rotterdam sweeps by the neighbourhood. A rather monumental housing block, nicknamed 'the ship', protects the collection of three-storey housing blocks from the street and contains most of the project's subsidized low-income apartment units.

In keeping with Prinsenland's overall plan, designers Francine Houben, Chris Weijer and Erik van Egeraat created a sense of a small-scale, almost attenuated and heavily planted public space between the buildings, while creating larger-scale greenswards to the northern and eastern edges. The rows of housing are mainly separated from each other with narrow alleyways giving onto small, individual gardens in front of the kitchens. In between the rows, gardens designed in French, English and Japanese styles provide clearly identifiable internal open space for the neighbourhood. They are also the most literal interpretation of the 'rooms' that Palmboom had asked for in his plan.

Shaped like waves of water, Mecanoo's blocks confirm the dominant geometric principles which Palmboom and Bakker had found and ordained as the base for development, while deforming them through the slight angles to create a sense of rhythm that is wholly Plasbuurt Oost's own. The buildings are constructed with standard technology and have internal layouts that do not differ much from contemporary developments. They confirm, in other words, existing housing technology and types. Yet the undulations create a sense of a distinct neighborhood.

Mecanoo then elaborated the three standard building types (row, crescent and 'ship') in highly complex compositions of brick, stucco, concrete and glass. The rows step up from north to south, presenting white-painted, rather monumental fronts to the north side, and reddish stucco façades to the south side. Concrete construction elements peek through to support overhangs and sills, giving the facades a sense of depth, while the bases on the garden sides are highly plastic in their detailing, exactly at the point where one enters and leaves one's dwelling.

The two curved buildings are covered with balconies, and have little identity of their own, at least in comparison with the almost extreme articulation of the rows to either side. The larger bar building, meanwhile, presents a closed mask to the larger world. It also revives the tradition of the housing block as presenting an image of fortress-like solidarity, while references to earlier 20th-century prototypes such as Bruno Taut's siedlungen in Berlin provide a coherent aesthetic. Its north and most public side is mainly covered in white stucco, though the eastern section, where it must help bring a sense of closure to the neighborhood, is painted dark grey. To the rear, the building's mass is broken down with a concrete grid containing the apartments' balconies.

What is most remarkable is the variety of scale the design achieves. The larger buildings conform to the scale and sweep of the major east-west artery and prepare the way for the larger and older apartment buildings to the east, while the small rows echo and transform into a modern idiom: the undulating lines of the original road running just beyond the new lake to the south. The planting scheme then intensifies this two-scale approach, while adding a third element, that of the four gardens, that is wholly the neighbourhood's own. The detailing of each building then reinforces the themes set in the overall design and makes them into usable and graspable forms.

As they have in much of their other work, Mecanoo here succeeded in transforming the aesthetic traditions of modernism, with their sliding geometries and clearly expressed planes, into a humanly scaled and gentler collection of forms that is still rooted in mass production building practises and recognizable housing types. The success of this particular project, however, is just as much the result of the way in which they responded to and honoured Prinsenland's larger planning decisions, which in and of themselves created a way for the reality of modern living to find a relation with the ground of the historically defined landscape in which that living takes place.

1994-2004
Ypenburg The Hague

Boswijk
De Bras
De Singels
De Venen
Waterwijk

almboom & Van den Bout **Urban plan, Ypenburg, design 1994, completion 1996-2008
2003 aerial photo)**

erial photograph from the west. North of the former runway lie the Singels, the most urban field, with a
reat deal of stacked housing construction. Northeast of this lies Boswijk, a luxury residential district in and
round the old camouflage woods and water elements, which have been retained. South of the Landings-
an lies the Waterwijk, an entirely newly developed water structure with large and small islands. The
rightly coloured dwellings by MVRDV show up as dots. The Venen and Bras fields are still to be developed.

Palmboom & Van de Bout collection, Rotterdam

Palmboom & Van den Bout **Urban plan, Ypenburg, design 1994, framework**

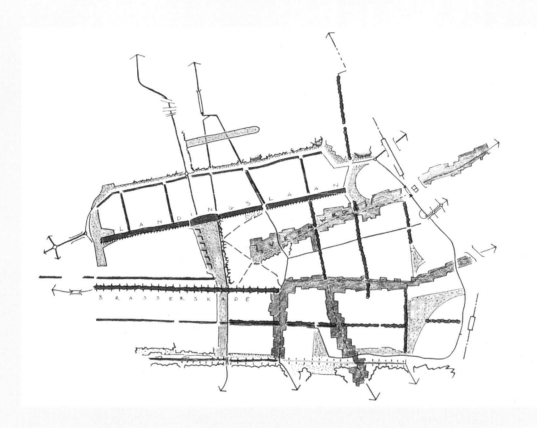

The masterplan is composed of a grid and fields. The framework gives the plan its structure and is composed of avenues and ribbons. The spine of the grid is the central axis, the Landingslaan, which runs through the plan as a reminder of the former runway.

Palmboom & Van den Bout **Urban plan, Ypenburg, design 1994, fields**

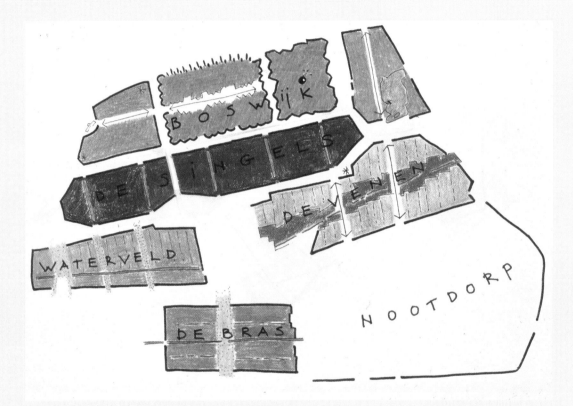

The five fields are components of the masterplan, each with its own characteristics. Designers of section plans were to be allowed to improvise within the five fields. 'Urban planning as a jam session' was how Palmboom described this construction.

Architecten Cie, Diener & Diener, Karelse Van der Meer Architecten, Topos Architecten **Sectio**
Plan 6, De Singels, 2001-2003, façades

West 8, urban design & landschape architecture collection, Rotterdam

The winning section plan six in the Singels field. The urban plan is by West 8, the architecture by Architecten Cie, Diener & Diener Architekten, Karelse van der Meer Architecten and Topos Architecten.

7X ac   6B ac   6A dd   6D km   6A dd   6C dd   6C dd   6C dd   6C dd   6D km   6D km   6A dd   6A dd   6B ac   6A dd   6B dd   6A dd   7E dd
Blok 11   Blok 10   Blok 9

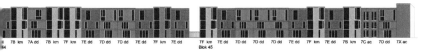

7B km   7A dd   7B km   7F km   7E dd   7D dd   7D dd   7E dd   7F km   7E dd   7F km   7E dd   7D dd   7D dd   7D dd   7E dd   7F km   7E dd   7B km   7C ac   7D dd   7X ac
                                                                    Blok 45

studio dd studio km6 km   3 km   1 to   1C to   3 ac   1 to   3 ac   3 ac   1 to   1C to   3 km   1 to   3 km   1C to   1 to   3 ac   3 ac   1 to   3 km   1 to   3 ac   3 km

3 km   3 ac   1e km   5 km   5 km   7E dd   7D dd   6 km   6 km   6B ac   studio dd studio dd   7d dd
Blok 31   Blok 32   Blok 36   Blok 37

6A dd   6C dd   6B ac   7B km   6A dd   7E dd   7A dd   7E dd   7B km   5 ac   5 ac   5 ac   5 ac   5 ac   5 ac   5 ac   studio km studio dd   7X dd
                                    Blok 5

1C to   1 to   1 to   3 km   studio dd   7X dd   7X ac   7X ac

7Q dd   Toren ac   4A to   4A to   5 ac   5 ac   3 ac   3 ac   3 ac   3 ac   1e km   3 ac   3 ac   3 km   3 I
Blok 56   Blok 55   Blok 54   Blok 53   Blok 52   Blok 49

MVRDV **Dwellings Hageneiland, 2000-2001 (2002 photo)**

photograph by Ralph Kämena

On Hageneiland cars have been banished to the outskirts of the island. Many houses are accessible only from the footpaths. The 37 rows of houses are alternately situated at the front, the centre or the rear of the parcels, so that there is no longer a hierarchy associated with the front or rear.

MVRDV **Dwellings Hageneiland, 2000-2001, collage**

MVRDV collection, Rotterdam

The dwellings have an archetypal form: they are the kind of houses a child would draw. The exterior – façades and roofs – is entirely clad in a single type of material in a single colour.

MVRDV **Dwellings Hageneiland, 2000-2001, collage**

MVRDV collection, Rotterdam

The public paths are planted with hedges and are paved with gravel.

D. van Gameren / Architectengroep **Dwellings, Section Plan 2, De Singels, 2002**

photograph by Christian Richters

**The winning section plan two in the Singels field north of the Landingslaan.
The urban planning and architectural design of the western section is by D. van
Gameren of De Architectengroep.**

D. van Gameren / Architectengroep **Dwellings, Section Plan 2, De Singels, 2002**

photograph by Christian Richters

The roofs and walls of the dwellings are joined virtually seamlessly.

...rchitecten Cie, Diener & Diener, Karelse Van der Meer Architecten, Topos Architecten **Section Plan 6, De Singels,** ...001-2003, view on some of the realised projects

...ecause of the variation in building and storey heights, dwelling types and alignment, the buildings evoke ...gradually evolved streetscape in a historic city.

Ypenburg
Hans Ibelings

The Ypenburg VINEX district near The Hague is one of the large-scale housing locations in the Netherlands which have been under construction since the mid-1990s. The resolution to build these expansion districts is described in the Vierde Nota Extra (Fourth Report Extra), abbreviated as VINEX, the 1990 supplement to the Vierde Nota Ruimtelijke Ordening (Fourth National Policy Document on Spatial Planning).

Ypenburg stands on the former site of the similarly named airfield, which was still part of the municipalities of Rijswijk, Pijnacker and Nootdorp when development commenced in the mid-1990s. In 2001, the district was annexed by The Hague. Designed to an urban masterplan by Palmboom & Van den Bout, it covers about 600 hectares where, towards the end of the first decade of this century, about 12,000 homes will have been built on 340 hectares. In addition, the district includes 85 hectares of business park and 7,000 square metres of retail space. The remaining 170 hectares are expanses of green and water, or roadway.

In recent years, the VINEX district has matured into a concept for contemporary suburban living with a generally negative tone. All the objections which might be raised against the suburbs constructed in the Netherlands since the Second World War are clumped together in the critique of the VINEX development: monofunctionality (almost exclusively living), uniformity (almost exclusively single-family dwellings) and sameness (almost 35 houses per hectare everywhere). The building density of the VINEX district is, moreover, neither one thing nor the other: too high for a rural living environment yet too low for a true city. The same applies for the location: too close to the city to be rural, yet too poorly connected with the city to belong to it.

All these criticisms could equally be levelled at Ypenburg, but given the fact that a VINEX district normally comprises 35 single-family dwellings per hectare, this is one of the better examples. If, within the strictures of modern-day housing production, there is somewhere that the full spectrum of suburban living for the middle classes is displayed then it is in Ypenburg. The district is shaped by a well-thought-out urban masterplan by Palmboom & Van den Bout, which provides a footing without being oppressive, includes sometimes wholly original urban planning elaborations of this masterplan, and features construction to a generally high architectural standard. In addition, a select group of designers has been involved in Ypenburg, including Architectuurstudio H. Hertzberger, Atelier Quadrat, P. Bedaux of Bedaux De Brouwer, J. Bosch, Claus en Kaan, F. van Dongen of de Architecten Cie, D. van Gameren of de architectengroep, Geurst en Schulze, Karelse & Van der Meer, K. Christiaanse's KCAP, S.V. Khandekar, Maccreanor & Lavington, Molenaar & Van Winden, Mulleners & Mulleners, MVRDV, Rapp & Rapp, R. Steenhuis, T. Koolhaas's TKA and A. Geuze's West 8.

In the 1994 urban masterplan, Palmboom & Van den Bout set out five residential areas in Ypenburg: Boswijk, De Singels, Waterveld, De Venen and De Bras. With 48 houses per hectare, density is highest in de Singels. This is where the highest proportion of stacked housing is found. Boswijk, Ypenburg's villa neighbourhood, has only 14 houses per hectare. De Venen has slightly above than the average density of 35 dwellings per hectare; Waterwijk and De Bras slightly less. One stipulation was that 30 per cent of the housing would be inexpensive, 45 per cent would be mid-price and 25 per cent expensive.

The five areas, which have each been imbued with a unique atmosphere and character, are subdivided into a total of 20 sector plans. Commissions were awarded immediately for the elaboration of three of these plans; one sector has, for the meantime, been left blank. For the centre area and the other 15 sectoral plans with housing, competitions were held for consortia of developers and teams of designers in 1996.

Thanks to the orchestrated three-step variation, there are differences between Ypenburg's five areas, within those areas, and also within the sectoral plans. Nowadays that is a fairly common approach in order to deal with the lack of design prompts. Where the context and the uniform housing programme offer no starting-points for a design, the theming of the urban plan often offers a way out. The multiplication of the number of architectonic expressions is now a frequently applied technique to avoid each street and each house looking exactly like the next one or the one before. The Kattenbroek district in Amersfoort, a design by A. Bahlotra of Kuiper Compagnons, offers one of the earliest and also most extreme examples of this means of gaining a grip on the literal and figurative emptiness that precedes an expansion project. In Kattenbroek, for fear of dullness, everything is subjected to an inescapable (and poetic) theme. In districts like Ypenburg, the thematic dictates do not go beyond a subtle hint of the atmosphere of the public space and the architectural character within each of the five areas. Thanks to that restraint, Ypenburg has not been subjected to some glaringly obvious similarity between sectoral plans within an area. The themes have, however, at least given the designers involved a design prompt, which was otherwise absent from the context and the required residential programmes.

The fact that the majority of floor plans for housing in Ypenburg do not deviate from standard typologies has partly to do with the levelling effects of market demand: satisfying this inevitably leads to solu-tions more mediocre than extreme. Additionally, it seems as if the single-family dwelling has now been developed to such an extent that innovations are only still possible in secondary areas and details.

The relatively great visual variation that has been achieved in the architecture of Ypenburg nevertheless is primarily thanks to the liberties that designers have taken in the small domain remaining to them in contemporary housing construction: exterior and subdivision of the plots. In terms of style, the architecture of Ypenburg embraces both the delicate neo-traditionalism of Molenaar & Van Winden and the hip, photogenic 'Monopoly' houses by MVRDV. The architectural forms range from traditional terraces and blocks to their whimsically deformed interpretation by D. van Gameren, from the iron-willed concatenation of individual houses in the section by West 8 to the houses with gardens on the opposite side of the road by Claus en Kaan. Ypenburg, where 85 percent of dwellings are ground-access, has therefore not ended up an endless plain of uniform rows of single-family units, semi-detached and detached houses, but a varied sampler of suburban living in around the year 2000.

1918-2004
The future in plans

The Netherlands
Amsterdam and environs
Haarlemmermeerpolder
Rotterdam
Het Groene Hart

J. London **Study for the ideal city, 'Lichtstad', 1918, plan**

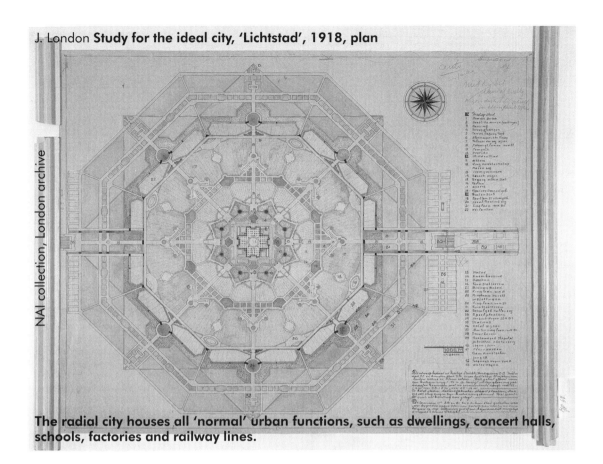

The radial city houses all 'normal' urban functions, such as dwellings, concert halls, schools, factories and railway lines.

J. London **Study for the ideal city, 'Lichtstad', 1918, sacred city with temple of brotherhood**

The decision to use an oriental architecture style is a striking aspect of this design. Domes and other comparable style elements are also found in this period in the work of Berlage, for example.

H.Th. Wijdeveld **Study for 'Chaos and Order' expansion plan, Amsterdam 1920-1927,
residential tower blocks lining boulevard to Haarlem-Zandvoort**

NAI collection, London archive

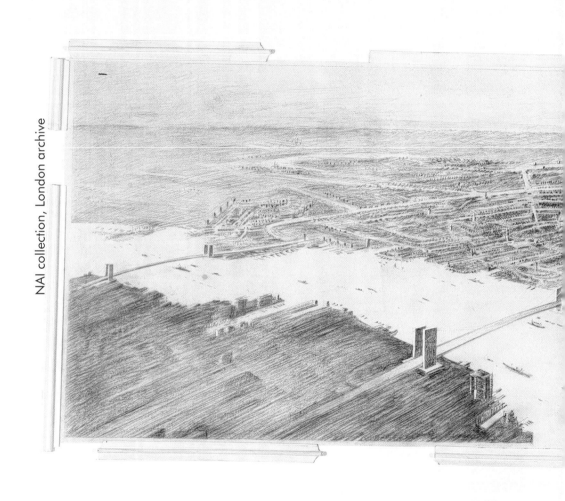

**In 1927 H.Th. Wijdeveld produced a reasonably feasible design for the Allebéplein
for Berlage's Plan Zuid. However, this design was not implemented. The same year
he devoted himself to another visionary plan: a double bridge over the IJ. The design
attests to an unceasing ambition to achieve the quasi-impossible.**

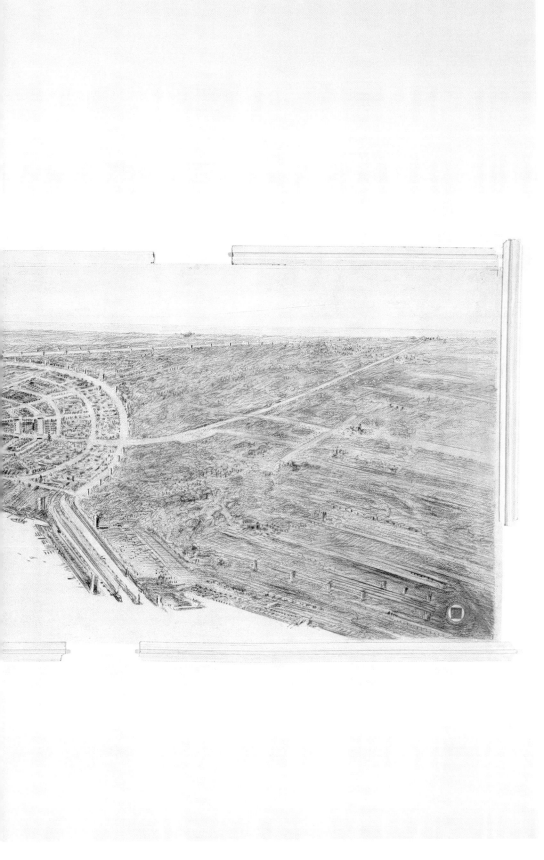

H.Th. Wijdeveld **Study for 'Chaos and Order' expansion plan, Amsterdam 1920-1927, residential tower blocks lining boulevard to Haarlem-Zandvoort**

NAI collection, Wijdeveld archive

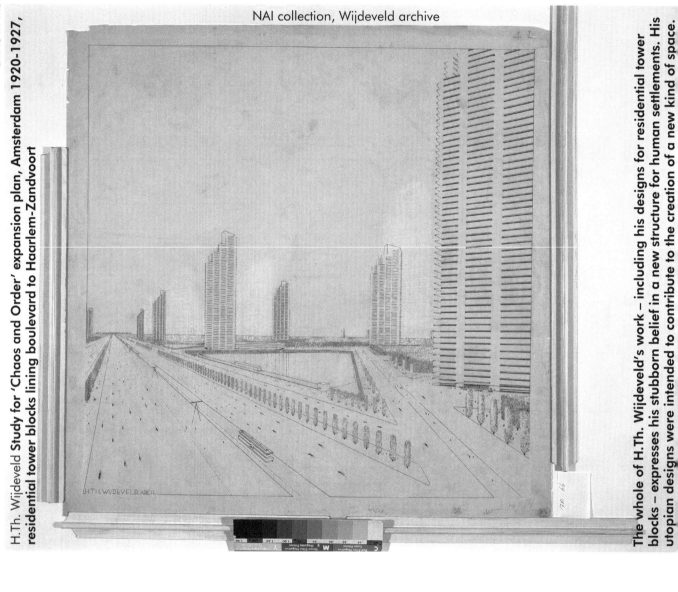

The whole of H.Th. Wijdeveld's work – including his designs for residential tower blocks – expresses his stubborn belief in a new structure for human settlements. His utopian designs were intended to contribute to the creation of a new kind of space.

he vision of the future for the expansion of Amsterdam is based on an earlier plan for the Vondelpark.
f the city continues to grow according to a radical and orderly structure, and housing is concentrated in
partment blocks, sufficient space is left over for parks.

J.B. Bakema, H. Klopma / Van den Broek en Bakema **Study for Pampus expansion plan, Amsterdam, 1964-1965, maquette of the four islands in the direction of Amsterdam**

NAI collection, Van den Broek en Bakema archive

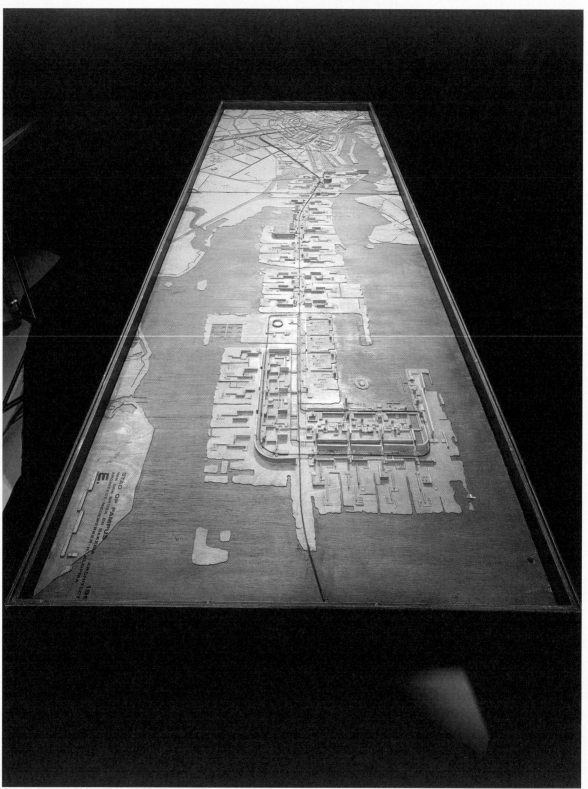

In the expansion area of Amsterdam, 350,000 people are supposed to be able to live and work. The contrast between this accumulation of people and the emptiness of the IJmeer is significant. As a comparison, when IJburg is completed in 2012, 45,000 people will be living on seven islands in the IJmeer.

J. Bakema, H. Klopma **Study for Pampus expansion plan, Amsterdam 1964-1965, view from office tower on central arterial street**

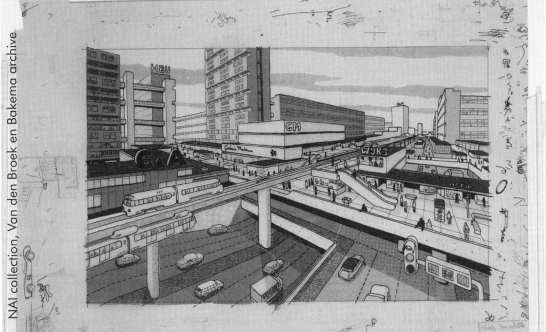

NAI collection, Van den Broek en Bakema archive

Along the central axis, the 'energy line', buildings feature a maximum of 40 storeys. Within this, shops, offices and dwellings are planned, guaranteeing the independent character of this expansion area of Amsterdam.

J. Bakema, H. Klopma **Study for Pampus expansion plan, Amsterdam 1964-1965, view from residential balcony onto centre of residential neighbourhood**

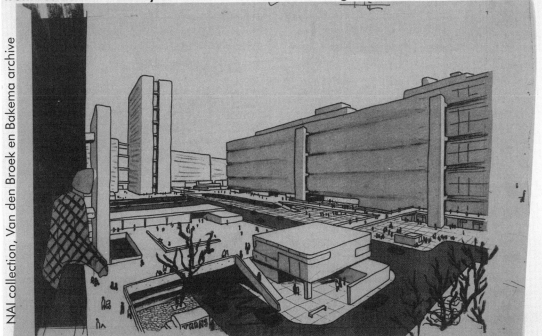

NAI collection, Van den Broek en Bakema archive

The architect Bakema was convinced that the large dimensions of Pampus fit the dimensions of the landscape. The mega-structure, according to him, was the only solution for the future urbanization of the Netherlands.

J. Bakema, H. Klopma **Study for Pampus expansion plan, Amsterdam, 1964-1965, view from residential balcony onto yacht marina and the IJ**

NAI collection, Van den Broek en Bakema archive

The ambition of Van den Broek and Bakema was to combine a high concentration of residents with a sense of space and nature available within easy reach.

R. Koolhaas, K. Christiaanse / Office for Metropolitan Architecture **Study, 'Agro-industry in the Haarlemmermeer', 1986-1987, maquette of total plan**

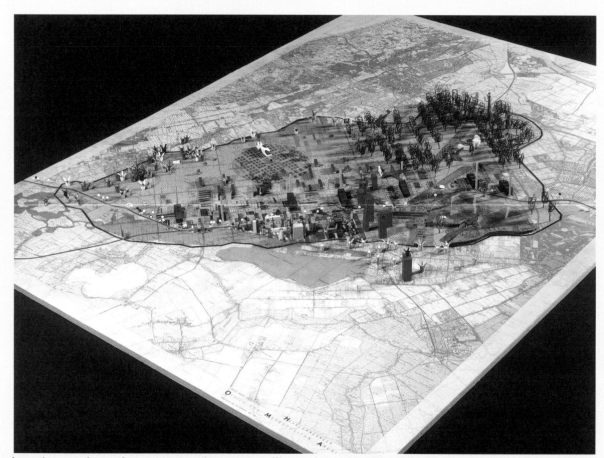

Future housing and employment requirements will result in steadily greater concentration densities. Yet building will take place in relatively empty areas such as the Groene Hart as well. This plan antici-pates these inevitable developments.

R. Koolhaas, K. Christiaanse / Office for Metropolitan Architecture **Study, 'Agro-industry in the Haarlemmermeer', 1986-1987, associative atmosphere picture**

NAI collection, Office for Metropolitan Architecture archive

'One of the qualities of the Dutch polder landscape is that its rational parcel allocation makes it a highly suited foundation on which to house different programmes, and at the same time presents a fairly constant characteristic landscape picture.'

R. Koolhaas, K. Christiaanse / Office for Metropolitan Architecture **Study, 'Agro-industry in the Haarlemmermeer', 1986-1987, associative atmosphere picture**

NAI collection, Office for Metropolitan Architecture archive

The design involves an accumulation of housing, employment, transport systems and leisure. The expansive 'carpet-metropolis' that emerges offers a new form of urban environment, which unfolds outside the existing urban cores.

A. Geuze **Study, 'Wilderness, a conceptual experiment for the empty space in the Randstad', 1993,
associative impression of the living environment of the 'contemporary city-dweller'**

**The standard dwelling is devaluated in A. Geuze's plan to merely one of several inhabitable options.
Other options present themselves, such as water towers, former farmhouses or warehouses.**

Geuze **Study, 'Wilderness, a conceptual experiment for the empty space in the Randstad', 1993,** associative impression of the living environment of the 'contemporary city-dweller'

NAI collection, Architecture International Rotterdam archive

project 'Wilderness' fits in a design outlook that typifies a younger generation of Dutch designers. actual construction is not the ultimate goal. The core of the work is rather the conceptual analysis d extrapolation of data.

From city of light to carpet metropolis
JaapJan Berg

The question of how people will be living in the near or more distant future is constant and fundamental in nature. Lifestyle and housing are, after all, such a pivotal element in our lives that many of us think about this issue, almost instinctively. Visions of the future, whether or not they are described or portrayed as fictive, can offer an inspiring spectrum of potential answers. Within the context of architecture and urban planning, imagining the future often sparks intriguing suggestions and ideas.

Within these visions of the future it is possible to draw a distinction between plans which present a plausible future and those which propose a sublime Utopia. The first category of plan, a design vision, is rooted in the reality of today, and therefore often includes recognizable elements. Existing data and givens are used as the launch pad for proposing a plausible vision of the future, near or distant. Future scenarios of this kind play an important role in deciding on long-term spatial policy.

Another category, Utopia, represents a much more extreme and improbable projection into the future. These plans are often received as cultural expressions, and their designers seldom or never harbour the illusion that they will actually be realized. There is, generally, more attention to and consideration for the design vision and the Utopia in the disciplines of architecture and urban planning than is the case for cultural visions in, say, cinema or literature. The reason for this lies partly in the fact that such architectonic visions are conceived and sketched by designers who must be considered capable of producing something realizable. For example, many design visions are realistically executable, and in practice designers often combine the production of visions of this kind with projects that are actually realized, projects that are currently feasible. That synthesis within a single being or oeuvre establishes credibility that a filmmaker or author often lacks.

The disadvantage of visions of the future is, of course, that they cannot be assessed in reality – they are not realized – and this is one reason why they could relatively easily be set aside as irrelevant. Despite that paper-bound status they are still valuable, for one because real-life data, elements and information serve as a starting point for the conception of the images. That direct relationship between reality and future is, moreover, characteristic of Dutch architects. Designs by architects such as London, Wijdeveld,

Van den Broek en Bakema, Koolhaas and Geuze offer a glimpse of the future in its various guises and simultaneously – perhaps even more emphatically – an impression of the age in which they are designed. The fact that they are, at best, rarely built or realized is not really significant. Design visions are an enduring shadow of the built reality and are thus inextricably and inevitably linked with it.

At the start of the 20th century, the far-reaching consequences of the Russian Revolution, the First World War and the progressive industrialization in the Western world created a chaotic situation that many believed could only be resolved by new hierarchies, systems and ideologies. The writer F. van Eeden (1860-1932) was one of these thinkers, and attempted to imagine a better future. In Het Godshuis in de Lichtstad ('The House of God in the City of Light'), published in 1921, he unfolded his socialist-utopian dreams and semi-mystical urban ideal. His argument was clearly directed against the existing cities, which he saw as 'morbid excrescences ... built as if by accident, under the influence of base inclinations, of lust for profit and advantage, for prosperity ....' His alternative for these urbane tumours, the 'City of Light', expresses an idealistically tinged faith in a future that would be harmonious, well-ordered and in equilibrium. All the functions in this city of the future, including living, are rigidly arranged in a pattern of various rings around the centrally set place of worship or temple building. Van Eeden's design provides for a circular 'well-organized congregation of at least 100,000 permanent residents' arranged in three sections with functions that become 'holier and increasingly sacral' the closer they are to the centre. Apart from that, the design is also thorough in providing for all imaginable urban functions and spaces, such as banks, ports and 'stations for air-ship transport'. The author left the visual elaboration of this ideal city to the Dutch architect J. London (1872-1953). In the drawings included in the publication, the most remarkable, besides the perfectly radial city plan, are the oriental, stylized buildings with, for example, dome-shaped roofs. The visionary design by Van Eeden and London is a reflection of, on the one hand, the reality at that time and, on the other, an illustration of Van Eeden's pursuit of political and social order and a depiction of his ideals and expectations. Van Eeden compared his plan with designs by K.P.C. de Bazel and, more specifically, with H. P. Berlage's design for the Pantheon der Mensheid ('Pantheon of Mankind'). Berlage designed this peace monument in 1915, during the First World War, in the spirit of the pacifism and internationalism of that era.

This social idealism calls to mind another much more recent and renowned design for an ideal city of the future. From 1960, the artist C. Nieuwenhuys (b. 1920), better known under his first name, Constant, developed the design for the urban structure of 'New Babylon'. Constant was not an architect by profession, was a founding member of the Situationist International movement to which the French philosopher G. Debord also adhered.

The Situationist International strove, among other things, to envisage a dynamic urbanism which could respond to current and influential developments in society, such as population growth, leisure activities and technological innovations. New Babylon proposed a flexible city which could be reconfigured at will, providing the backdrop for play, experience and inventiveness. The inhabitants are liberated from work and have therefore become homo ludens, the playful human.

That this societal consciousness underlies the design is evident from Constant's explanation of it: 'The urban plan is the expression and the image of the societal structure, and one can effect no essential change in it without first changing society.' As with Van Eeden and London, for Constant's Babylon the architectonic design was determined by the societal reality, but even more by idealistic expectations for the future. In these visions of the future, the domestic architecture serves only to illustrate these ideas and loses credibility because it is not first of all designed by architects. Both these examples are sooner Utopia than visionary design.

The design visions by the expressionist architect T. Wijdeveld (1885-1987) also sprung from a critical analysis of society, especially of existing cities and use of space. Wijdeveld's plans seem, however, to have been designed to be feasibly constructed. With him, the gap between future and reality was thus narrower, even though his credo of chasing the impossible seemed to repeatedly produce an unbridgeable chasm between intention and reality. He therefore stood opposite the realism and functionalism of designers of the Nieuwe Zakelijkheid, literally 'New Objectivity', the Dutch functionalist movement aligned with the International Modern style. Wijdeveld's study for the 'Chaos and order' expansion plan of Amsterdam (1920-1927) proposed a linear urban plan with an important place for high-rise flats. The design of these flats is reminiscent of the 1921 design by L. Mies van der Rohe for a glass skyscraper on the Friedrichstrasse in Berlin. Both designs consist of transparent flats with apparently gravity-defying floors, and embody the expected mass public housing of the future. The biggest expansion plan by Wijdeveld initially stretched to the North Sea coastline, and in 1954 and 1960 he extended it even further with two designs for expansion into the sea, which meant the city would reach almost to infinity.

Unlike Van Eeden and London, Wijdeveld's creation of his design vision was based on an analysis of the existing city of Amsterdam and not of 'the city in general'. According to this architect, the growth pattern of Amsterdam would in future lead to chaos. As a forewarning, he depicts this in his design, with his alternative of a radical, radial plan alongside. The design vision presents a 'mega housing problem' that cannot be solved with the existing system229 atics of urbanism and residential architecture. Wijdeveld envisaged a 'city-free future', a new structure for human settlement in which the living environment and landscape would spill over into one another.

It is striking that the residential landscape proposed by Wijdeveld resurfaced later, albeit in a different guise, in a design by the landscape architect A. Geuze (b. 1960). Geuze drafted a design for the future urbanization of Rotterdam's Alexanderpolder in 1993, in the context of the manifestation 'AIR-Alexander: New Urban Frontiers'. This multidisciplinary event gave various designers and artists the opportunity to interpret and provide commentary on this process. That is illustrative of a tendency that gained sway during the final decades of the twentieth century. Design exercises and ideas competitions therefore increasingly lead to the abandonment of conventions and rules that had proven overly restrictive in the actual process of designing a residential neighbourhood or a city. Geuze's plan envisaged a spectacular urbanization of the Alexanderpolder and the adjacent 'Green Heart'. The existing Alexanderpolder neighbourhood was designed in the 1950s by L. Stam-Beese and J. Bakema, who were aligned with the CIAM movement at the time. Their plan also proposed that expansion of the neighbourhood moved towards, into the landscape. Geuze's plan isolates the neighbourhood expansion from the existing city of Rotterdam in a much more radical manner, and proposes further development and construction in the Green Heart. The plan for the Alexanderpolder is thus a representative fragment of the future inhabited landscape of the entire Randstad.

For Geuze, the Green Heart formed a space or void which he wanted to colonize with an estimated one million houses, to be constructed in varying densities. The most marked difference with Wijdeveld's 'Chaos and order' expansion plan for the park city is the degree of densification that Geuze had in mind. Whereas Wijdeveld showed a preference for widely dispersed high-rise construction,

Geuze opted for an extensive and new urban wilderness composed of differentiated housing types, a multiplicity of densities and cultures. The inhabitant of this wilderness, the 'modern urbanite', is a self-assured, inquisitive and mobile individual who lives, works and recreates at all kinds of different places within that territory and the existing cores round about.

Geuze effectively designed a living landscape where existing principles and models no longer apply. It aims to present an alternative for the undifferentiated strategy that is usually the basis for deciding building sites and space where construction is forbidden. After all, many urban expansion areas are executed according to a mindless copy-and-paste principle. Geuze's design is a good example of a vision for the future as an experiment in philosophy and design. It offers a glimpse of a potential development based on an analysis and assessment of modern-day components. It is therefore part of a trend in which design visions for the living environment in the Netherlands increasingly revolve around use of space and population density (as well as the attendant consequences).

In the design vision sketched by OMA/R. Koolhaas and K. Christiaanse in 1986 for the development of the Haarlemmermeerpolder, the expected intensified use of the available space is also a core theme. They also turn their attention to part of the Green Heart – an area that has come under increasing pressure, in part because of plans like this kind, since there is a lack of certainty about the 'colour' of the future zoning. The design by Koolhaas and Christiaanse shifts the accent more to the anticipated tension between the poles of spatial claims for economic growth on the one hand and housing on the other. The design for agro-industry in the Haarlemmermeer foresees a massive intensification of industrial and economic developments in an area that is primarily 'coloured' by agriculture. Koolhaas and Christiaanse proceeded from an infill of the Haarlemmermeer between 1986 and 2050 in which agro-industry predominates. These architects believe that farming will in future no longer be land-bound or dependent on daylight. Their plan limits residential functions to existing cores and a number of country estates.

These residential functions, and others, are placed within a bigger structure. The architectural detailing is distinctly left blank. In an accompanying text, the designers argue that the architect can never imagine the various architectural styles of the future without lapsing into science-fiction or kitsch. Like the plans by Wijdeveld and Geuze, the design by Koolhaas and Christiaanse presumes an ineluctable urban densification in the Netherlands. Each of these three designs opts for a kind of symbiosis between landscape and living environments and appeal for a new urbanity. This plan includes a collage of all kinds of different functions within an area around traffic and transport hubs, especially Amsterdam's Schiphol Airport. That urbanization is emphatically set at the periphery of the extant, actual centre. In one of the collages of the design, the skyline of Amsterdam is tellingly set in the background. This vision is described as 'a collage of fragments, an extended urban landscape, the carpet metropolis' and is based on a stacking of work, living and recreation programmes.

This concept has been frequently and variously applied in designs which analyse the current and future use of space in the Netherlands. MVRDV, for example, has interpreted it extremely literally in their design for the spectacular Dutch Pavilion for the World Expo in Hanover in 2000 and – more in the line of agro-industry – in the vision of stacked industrial pig-rearing in Pig City. The plan by Koolhaas and Christiaanse was devised in the frame-work of the 'Nederland Nu als Ontwerp' ('The Netherlands Now as Design') manifestation, an exhibition and discussion platform which was organized by the foundation of the same name between 1985 and 1987 in order to prevent the Netherlands falling into a laid-back complacency and to stimulate it to think about its future. This event is now considered one of the milestones in the history of Dutch thinking on the future of living, working and recreation. Besides OMA, other participants in 'Nederland Nu als Ontwerp' included designers such as T. Koolhaas, H. de Boer, P. de Bruin, A. Hosper, Benthem/Crouwel, C. Weeber and Mecanoo/F. Houben. Whether the design visions of Koolhaas, Christaanse and Geuze will ever become reality is perhaps a question of time. The future of the Green Heart and the issues of a shortage of space and population density are still hot topics, for designers as well as in the political arena. Moreover, the possibility of realizing a design vision cannot be completely excluded – and that is an additional reason to study such scenarios carefully. In addition to the embedding in reality noted above, that inherent possibility of realization prevents such projections being all too simplistically neutered as unrealistic, subjective and innocent ideas.

A good example of this is the urban study for Pampus by the Rotterdam-based Van den Broek en Bakema architecture bureau. This design vision for living was at one time set aside as undesirable and unfeasible, yet in a revised form it still made a comeback. The 1964 design proposed a linear city in the IJmeer lake, intended as an expansion neighbourhood for Amsterdam. No fewer than 350,000 people were meant to work and live there, more than a third of Amsterdam's present population. Pampus was a highpoint in the work of Van den Broek en Bakema, and was in fact a follow-up to earlier studies, for Pendrecht and Alexanderpolder, for example. The plan by J. Bakema and H. Klopma proposed an autonomous city on four interlinked islands of various shape. They were interconnected by an 'energy line' of arterial roads and a monorail. People would live in large (core) buildings of 15 to 40 storeys set along the central track/roadway. The architects hoped that elongated, narrow form of the islands would give the residents a sense of 'living in the city in the countryside'.

Though the Pampus plan was never realized in this proposed form, now, 30 years later, the IJburg expansion project is under construc-tion at the same location. The similarities are greater than might be apparent at first glance: IJburg is also composed of numerous islands in various forms; it also has a main axis with a tramway to the centre of the existing city; also here the objective is to create an urban residential environment in which the advantages of living outside the city must remain prominent. This extraordinary oppor-tunity to compare a historic design vision with a realized living environment sheds new light on both. The design by Van den Broek en Bakema gains a new topicality, stimulating interest in this historic design vision. At the same time, a new neighbourhood like IJburg, created from layers of spouted sand, can unexpectedly boast an historical background.

The designs by Wijdeveld, Geuze, Koolhaas/Christiaanse and Van den Broek en Bakema illustrate how general thought about and design of the future in the Netherlands is often directed by the continuing increase in use and exploitation of a relatively small and densely populated territory. As a consequence of this pressure and the stacking of activities and functions, there is a constant need for visions and solutions for this use of space. In 1997, the project 'De Nieuwe Kaart van Nederland' ('The New Map of the Netherlands') made a seminal, handsome compilation of the seemingly somewhat chaotic multitude of plans in the Netherlands. This map inexorably and simultaneously reveals all the projects and spatial claims that the various layers of government have planned from then through 2005. That continuous laying claim to space creates a certain eagerness for visionary plans. It is, in any case, the world of politics which often decides the decisive metamorphosis from design vision to reality. The faith in the 'makeability' and the oft-proclaimed 'artificiality' of the Netherlands play an important and significant role in this metamorphosis. Unlike most other countries, the Netherlands is the tangible product of concretely realized, now-historical visionary plans, such as the various land reclamation projects and the Delta Works storm surge barrier. That elementary coupling between reality and visions of the future at work in a symphonic combination with the proud tradition of engineering genius marks the Netherlands as a prime example of a land of the realized Utopia.

Literature
Authors
Acknowlegdements

General

Bergvelt, E., F. van Burkom and K. Gaillard (ed.), *Van neorenaissance tot postmodernisme. Honderdvijfentwintig jaar Nederlandse interieurs 1870-1995*, Rotterdam 1996

Bouw C. and R. Oldenziel (ed.), *Schoon genoeg. Huisvrouwen en huishoudtechnologie in Nederland 1898-1998*, Nijmegen 1998

Cieraad, I. and J. Hulsman, *Honderd jaar wonen in Nederland 1900-2000*, Rotterdam 2000

Fuhring P. and R. Eggink, *Binnenhuisarchitectuur in Nederland 1900-1981*, The Hague 1981

Grinberg D., *Housing in the Netherlands*, Delft 1977

Haan, J. de, *Villaparken in Nederland. Een onderzoek aan de hand van het villapark Duin en Dael te Bloemendaal 1897-1940*, Haarlem 1986

Klerk, L. de and H. Moscoviter, *En dat al voor de arbeidende klasse. 75 jaar volkshuisvesting Rotterdam*, Rotterdam 1992

Luning Prak, N., *Het Nederlandse woonhuis 1800-1940*, Delft 1990

Montijn, I., *Leven op stand 1890-1940*, Amsterdam 1998

Rijk, T. de, *Het elektrische huis. Vormgeving en acceptatie van elektrische huishoudelijke apparaten in Nederland*, Rotterdam 1998

Rossum, H. van, F. van Wijk and L. Baljon, *De stad in uitersten.Verkenningstocht naar VINEX-land*, Rotterdam 2001

Vreeze, N. de, *Woningbouw, inspiratie en ambities. Kwalitatieve grondslagen van de sociale woningbouw in Nederland*, Almere 1993

Vreeze, N. de (ed.), *6,5 miljoen woningen. 100 jaar woningwet en wooncultuur in Nederland*, Rotterdam 2001

Vondelstraat

Hellenberg Hubar, B. van, *Arbeid en bezieling. De esthetica van P.J.H. Cuypers, J.A. Alberdingk Thijm en V.E.L. de Stuers*, Nijmegen 1997

Hoogewoud, G., *P.J.H. Cuypers en Amsterdam*, The Hague 1985

Keuning, D. and L. Lansink, *A.L. van Gendt, J.G. van Gendt, A.D.N. van Gendt. Architecten in zaken*, Rotterdam 1999

Maeyer, J. de and L. Verpoest (ed.), *Gothic Revival. Religion, Architecture and Style in Western Europe 1815-1914*, Leuven 2000

Oxenaar, A., 'Op zoek naar een schilderachtig straatbeeld. De stadswoonhuizen van P.J.H. Cuypers in de Vondelstraat (1867-1871)', in: J. Baart, *Amsterdam het be-schouwen waard*, Amsterdam 1993, 75-87

Valk, A. van der, *Amsterdam in aanleg. Planvorming en dagelijks handelen 1850-1900*, Amsterdam 1989

Wagenaar, M., *Amsterdam 1876-1914. Economisch herstel, ruimtelijke expansie en de veranderende ordening van het stedelijk grondgebruik*, Amsterdam 1990

Philipsdorp

Otten, A., *Philips' woningbouw 1900-1940. Fundament van woningstichting Hertog Hendrik van Lotharingen*, Zaltbommel 1991

Reinink, W., *K.P.C. de Bazel, Architect*, Rotterdam 1993 (second printing).

Betondorp

Bocanet, A., T. Boersma and L. Hermans (ed.), *Betondorp 1923-1987, gebouwd/verbouwd*, Amsterdam 1987

Boersma, T., *Betondorp, ontwerp, maatschappij, techniek*, Amsterdam 1987

Bruyn, W.J., 'Leven in een tuindorp. Enkele indicaties voor een waardering', *Forum*, 1965/66, no. 5-6, pp. 26-50

Eerenbeemt, S. van den, 'Betondorp ook nu weer model voor vergelijkbare complexen', *Renovatie & Onderhoud*, 1987, no. 12, pp. 16-21

Kuipers, M.C., *Bouwen in beton, experimenten in de volkshuisvesting voor 1940*, Den Haag 1987

Kuipers, M.C., 'Renovatie van innovatie, betondorpen in onderhoud', in: E.J. Nusselder (ed.), *Instandhouding, Jaarboek Monumentenzorg 1999*, Zwolle/Zeist 1999, pp. 118-127

Laar, F. van de, *Zeg nou zelf, dit is toch het mooiste plekje van heel Betondorp?*, Amsterdam 1988

Ottens, E., *Ik moet naar een kleinere woning omzien want mijn gezin wordt te groot*, Amsterdam 1975

Pennink, P.K.A., 'Het Betondorp', *Forum*, 1965/66, no. 5-6, pp. 8-23

Roegholt, R., *Amsterdam in de 20e eeuw, deel 1 (1919/1945)*, Utrecht/Antwerp 1976

Siraa, H.T., *Een miljoen nieuwe woningen*, The Hague 1989

Smit, F. *De Droom van Howard. Het verleden en de toekomst van de tuindorpen*, Rijswijk 1990

Plan Zuid

Bock, M., S. Johannisse and V. Stissi, Michel de Klerk. *Bouwmeester en tekenaar van de Amsterdamse School*, Rotterdam 1996

Bolhuis, G., *De atlas Gordel 20-40*, Amsterdam 2000

Buurman, M. and M. Kloos, *Godin van de Zuidas. De Minervalaan – as in tijd en ruimte*, Amsterdam 1999

Casciato, M., *De Amsterdamse School*, Rotterdam 1991

Fraenkel, F., *Het plan Amsterdam-Zuid van H.P. Berlage*, Amsterdam 1976

Gaillard, K. and B. Dokter (ed.), *Berlage en Amsterdam Zuid*, Rotterdam 1992

Kohlenbach, B., Pieter Lodewijk Kramer 1881-1961. *Architect van de Amsterdamse School*, Naarden 1994

Polano, S., *Hendrikus Petrus Berlage. Het complete werk*, Alphen aan de Rijn 1988

Searing, H., *Amsterdam-South: Social-democracy's elusive housing ideal*, Cambridge, Mass. 1988

Stieber, N., *Housing design and society in Amsterdam. Reconfiguring urban order and identity 1900-1920*, Chicago 1998

Hilversum

Bergeijk, B. van, *Willem Marinus Dudok. Architect-stedebouwkundige 1884-1974*, Naarden 1995

Bergeijk, H. van, 'Willem Marinus Dudok, an Architect and a Municipal Official', *Rassegna*, no. 75, 1998, pp. 52-69

Grinberg, D.I., *Housing in the Netherlands 1900-1940*, Delft 1982

Japelli, P and G. Menna, Willem Marinus Dudok. *Architetture e cittá 1884/1974*, Naples 1997

Langmead, D., *Willem Marinus Dudok. A Dutch Modernist*, Westport/London 1996

Scheffler, K., *Holland*, Leipzig 1930

Kiefhoek

Bakema, J.B., 'Architect Oud 5 april 1963 †', *Forum*, 1963, no. 17, p. 2

Cusveller, S., *De Kiefhoek een woonwijk te Rotterdam*, Laren 1990

Hoeven, E. van der, *J.J.P. Oud en Bruno Taut; ontwerpen voor een nieuwe stad Rotterdam-Berlijn*, Rotterdam 1993

Oud, H.E., *J.J.P. Oud. Architekt 1890-1963. Feiten en herinneringen gerangschikt*, The Hague 1984

Oud, J.J.P., 'Eine städtische Siedlung in Rotterdam', *Der Baumeister*, 1930, no. 28, p. 11

Oud, J.J.P., 'Die Städtische Siedlung "Kiefhoek" in Rotterdam', *Die Form*, 1931 no. 5, p. 14

Oud, J.J.P., 'Siedlung "Kiefhoek" in Rotterdam', *Zentralblatt der Bauverwaltung*, 1930, no. 51, p. 10

Oud, J.J.P., 'The £ 213 house', *The Studio*, 1931, p. 456

Polano, S., *Architettura Olandese. J.J.P. Oud*, Milan 1981

Stamm, G., *J.J.P. Oud. Bauten und Projekte 1906 bis 1963*, Mainz/Berlin 1984

Vletter, M. de, C. Wagenaar, D. Broekhuizen and E. Taverne, *J.J.P. Oud, Poëtisch functionalist 1890-1963, Compleet werk*, Rotterdam, 2001

Middelburg

Bleyenberg, W.H.M., 'Het herstel en de toekomst van de stad Middelburg' deel 1, *Polytechnisch Tijdschrift*, 1951, no. 3, pp. 45b-50b and 4, pp. 77b-83b

Bosma, K. (ed.), *Architectuur en stedebouw in oorlogstijd. De wederopbouw van Middelburg 1940-1948*, Rotterdam 1988

Bosma, K. and C. Wagenaar, *Een geruisloze doorbraak. De geschiedenis van architectuur en stedebouw tijdens de bezetting en de wederopbouw van Nederland*, Rotterdam 1995

Gids der voornaamste gemeenten van Nederland, meer in het bijzonder ten behoeve van hen, die zich in een dezer gemeenten wenschen te vestigen, Arnhem 1929

'Middelburg. Nieuwbouw aangepast aan bestaande bouwstijl', *Baksteen*, 1974, no. 5-6, pp. 33-37

Nederland in kaarten. Verandering van stad en land in vier eeuwen cartografie, Ede 1985

Ranitz, J. de, 'De wijze van voorbereiding en voorloopige resultaten van het streekplan Walcheren', *Tijdschrift voor Volkshuisvesting en Stedebouw*, 1940, no. 5, pp. 102-105 and 6, pp. 118-120

Sijmons, K.L., 'Middelburg', *Forum*, 1946 no. 3, pp. 86-88

Veur, M.W.G. van der, *Middelburg in oorlogs- en bezettingsjaren (1939-1944)*, Middelburg 1945

'De Wederopbouw van Nederland. Voordrachten, gehouden voor het Koninklijk Instituut van Ingenieurs in samenwerking met het Instituut voor Volkshuisvesting en Stedebouw, op 28 October 1940 te 's-Gravenhage', reprint from *De Ingenieur*, 1940, no. 52 and 1941, no. 3, 4 and 5, general section

Pendrecht

Damen, H. and A. Devolder, *Lotte Stam-Beese 1903-1988*, Rotterdam 1993

Dettingmeijer, R., *Het Nieuwe Bouwen in Rotterdam, 1920-1960*, Delft 1982

Klerk, L. de, *Particuliere plannen*, Rotterdam 1998

Mumford, E., *The CIAM discourse on urbanism 1928-1960*, Cambridge, Mass. 2000

Smolenaars, E., *Pendrecht (Stadsverhalen Rotterdam deel 3)*, Rotterdam 2001

Umberto Barbieri, S. (ed.), *Architectuur en planning. Nederland 1940-1980*, Rotterdam 1983

Wagenaar, C., *Welvaartsstad in wording. De wederopbouw van Rotterdam 1940-1952*, Rotterdam 1992

Woud, A. van der, *Het Nieuwe bouwen Internationaal: CIAM*, Delft 1983

Nagele

Andela, G., 'Nagele, lusthof voor het nieuwe bouwen', *Futura*, June 1982, pp. 2-23

Baart, Th., C. Markerink and A. van Veen, *Nagele*, Amsterdam 1988

'Bebouwing Wieringermeerpolder', *Tijdschrift voor stedebouw*, 1934, no. 1, pp. 4-7

Bruin, W., 'Over de dorpen van de Noordoostpolder', *Forum*, April 1955, p. 25

Constandse, A.K.C., 'Het dorp met de glamour', *Bouw*, 15 August 1964, pp. 1135-1139

Geluk, H., *Verbeelding in Flevoland: een nieuwe cultuur in een nieuwe provincie*, Amsterdam 1988

Hemel, Z. and V. van Rossem, *Nagele een collectief ontwerp 1947-1957*, Amsterdam 1984

Henselmans, M.A., *Nagele: stedebouw & architectuur: ontwerp & ontwikkelingsplan*, Nagele 1989

'Een plan voor het dorp Nagele', *Forum*, 1952, no. 6/7, pp. 172-178

Strauven, F. and A. van Eyck, *Relativiteit en verbeelding*, Amsterdam 1994

Wal, C. van der, *In praise of common sense. Planning the ordinary. A physical planning history of the new towns in the IJsselmeerpolders*, Rotterdam 1997

Wit, C. de, *Johan Niegeman 1902-1977*, Amsterdam 1979

Woensel, J.T.W.H. van, *Nieuwe dorpen op nieuw land: inrichting van de dorpen in Wieringermeer, Noordoostpolder, Oostelijk en Zuidelijk Flevoland*, Lelystad 1999

Voorhof

Boer, N. de, *De Randstad bestaat niet. De onmacht tot grootstedelijk beleid*, Rotterdam 1996

Embden, S.J. van, '....door die van een architect-stedebouwkundige', *Bouw*, 1960, pp. 434-437

Geest, J. van, S.J. van Embden. *Monografieën van Nederlandse stedenbouwkundigen*, Rotterdam 1996

Geest, J. van, 'Van woningnood en flatneurose naar luxe flatappartementen', in: N. de Vreeze (ed.), *6,5 miljoen woningen. 100 jaar woningwet en wooncultuur in Nederland*, Rotterdam 2001

Hellinga, H., Ernest Groosman. *Bouwer met grenzeloze ambities*, Rotterdam 2001

Hoog in Nederland, een onderzoek naar motieven achter hoogbouw, Amsterdam 1986

Laag of hoog bouwen en wónen? (Report of the commission on high-rise and low-rise buildings), The Hague 1961

Priemus, H., 'Wonen in de wolken', in: H. Priemus, Bouwen & Wonen. Inleiding in de woningbouw en volkshuisvesting, The Hague 1970

'Stad in het voorbijgaan', Bouw no. 7 (15 February 1964)

Wagenaar, M., 'Hoogbouw in het vlakke land. Hoge woongebouwen en kantoortorens in Holland, 1900-1992', *Holland, regionaal historisch tijdschrift*, 1992, pp. 270-286

Almere

Brouwer, P., *Van stad naar stedelijkheid. Planning en planconceptie van Lelystad en Almere 1969 – 1974*, Rotterdam 1997

Hemel, Z., *Het landschap van de IJsselmeerpolders. Planning, inrichting en vormgeving*, Rotterdam/The Hague 1994

Klingeren, F., *Zuidweststad. Woonlandschap*, Amsterdam 1970

Nawijn, K.E., *Almere. Hoe het begon. Achtergronden, herinneringen en feiten uit de eerste ontwikkelingsjaren van Almere*, Lelystad 1989

Provoost, M., B. Colenbrander and F. Alkemade, *Dutchtown. O.M.A.'s meesterproef in Almere*, Rotterdam 1999

Sande, J. van de (ed.), *Gewild Wonen: Bouwexpo Almere 2001*, Almere 2000

Stassen, B, and J.J. Berg, *Peetvaders van Almere. Interviews met bestuurders en ontwerpers*, Almere 2001

Stassen, B., *Bedacht en gebouwd. 25 jaar Almere Stad*, Almere 2001

Wal, C. van der, *In praise of common sense. Planning the ordinary. A physical planning history of the new town of the IJsselmeerpolders*, Rotterdam 1997

Nieuwmarkt Quarter

'..de beste aktiegroep ter wereld...', (Stichting De Oude Stad brochure), Amsterdam 1984

'Het Amsterdamse Nieuwmarktproject', in: F. Strauven, *Aldo van Eyck. Relativiteit en verbeelding*, Amsterdam 1984

Brouwers, R., '"Ik vind dat je juist in de binnenstad moet bouwen". Architect Theo Bosch over de Nieuwmarkt, de metro, de overloop en de geordende chaos', *Vrij Nederland*, 7 December 1974

Cate, F. ten, 'Wederneerhaalplan'. In: F. ten Cate, *Dit volckje seer verwoet: Een geschiedenis van de Sint Antoniebreestraat*, Amsterdam 1988, pp. 61-88

Eyck, A. van and Th. Bosch, *Beschrijving en Toelichting Stedebouwkundig plan reconstructiegebied Nieuwmarkt*, Amsterdam 1980 (revised 16 February 1981)

Heeswijk, H. van and P. de Ley, 'Woningbouwprojecten in de Nieuwmarktbuurt te Amsterdam', *Bouw*, 23 November 1985, no. 24

'Nieuwmarkt', *Forum*, 1984, no. 4, p. 41

'De Nieuwmarkt als wingewest', *Vrij Nederland*, 20 May 1978

'Het Pentagon van Theo Bosch', in: S. Lebesque (ed.), *Voor Hedy d'Ancona, minister van cultuur 1989-1994*, Amsterdam 1994, pp. 6-7

'Themanummer Nieuwmarkt-Lastage', *Forum*, no. 23, 4 November 1970

Prinsenland

Projectteam Prinsenland, *Structuurschets Prinsenland: concept voor de toelichting op het bestemmingsplan Prinsenland*, Rotterdam, 1984

Houben, F., Mecanoo, *Compositie, contrast, complexiteit*, Rotterdam, 2001

Somer K., *Mecanoo Architecten*, Rotterdam, 1995

Brouwers R. (ed.), *Jaarboek Architectuur in Nederland 1993/1994, Yearbook Architecture in the Netherlands 1993/1994*, Rotterdam, 1994

Grünhagen, H., 'Een groene buurt met een hoge dichtheid: Ringvaartplasbuurt Oost', in: *Woningraad Magazine*, 1993, no. 1. pp. 20-23

Reijndorp, A., 'El pays de los infantes: hoe stedelijk is de nieuwe tuinwijk van Mecanoo?', in: *De Architect*, 1993, no. 6, 1993, pp. 66-75

Gazzaniga L., 'Mecanoo Quartiere Prinsenland Rotterdam', in: *Domus* 1993, no. 745, pp. 36-38

Ypenburg

Venema, H. (ed.), *Buitenplaats Ypenburg: Een bevlogen bouwlocatie*, Bussum 2000

MVRDV Stacking and Layering/Apilamiento y estratificación 1997-2002, El Croquis (2002) nr. 111, 126-155

West 8, Milan, 42-46

The future in plans

Bouman, O., *Op het breukvlak van twee millenia. Gedachten over architectuur*, Rotterdam 1999

Devolder, A., *De Alexanderpolder. Waar de stad verder gaat*, Bussum 1993

Eeden, F. van, *Het Godshuis in de lichtstad*, Amsterdam 1921

Evers, F. (ed.), *Het aanzien van Nederland: de woonwijk van de toekomst* (Jury report for the 2000 Bouwfondsprijs), Rotterdam 2000

Ibelings, H., *Van den Broek en Bakema 1948-1988. Architectuur en stedenbouw*, Rotterdam 2000

Cammen, H. van der (ed.), *Nieuw Nederland: onderwerp van ontwerp 2015 / Stichting Nederland Nu Als Ontwerp*, The Hague 1987

Nieuwenhuys, C., *New Babylon*, The Hague 1974

Tummers, N., 'De mise en scène van de architectuur: plan the impossible', *Bouwkundig Weekblad* no. 83, 1965

Wijdeveld, H.Th., *1885-1985 mijn eerste eeuw*, Oosterbeek 1985

Jean-Paul Baeten is an architecture historian. He works for the Collections department of the Netherlands Architecture Institute (NAI) in Rotterdam.

JaanJan Berg has been curator at the Netherlands Architecture Institute (NAI) in Rotterdam since 2001. He served as project leader for, among others, the exhibitions Latent Space, Gio Ponti – a world of design, and GeWoon Architectuur, the new permanent exhibition of the NAI. He studied art history at the University of Amsterdam and, among other things, initiated and served on the editorial staff of the journal *Simulacrum*. From 1997 to 2001 he worked as a senior coordinator at CASLa, the architecture centre in Almere. His publications include *Peetvaders van Almere* (2001).

Herman van Bergeijk is an architecture historian and works in the Architecture Faculty at the Delft University of Techonology. One of his recent publications is *De Steen van Berlage* (2003). He will soon publish a study of the work of Jan Wils and a book about the Märzgefallenendenkmal in Weimar (in association with K.J. Winkler).

Aaron Betsky is an architect, architecture historian and critic and director of the Netherlands Architecture Institute (NAI) in Rotterdam. From 1995 to 2001 he was curator of architecture, design and digital projects at the San Francisco Museum of Modern Art (SF-MOMA). His publications include such titles as *Architecture Must Burn* (2000), *Landscrapers* (2002) and *Three California Houses: The Homes of Max Palevsky* (2003).

Joosje van Geest is an architecture historian based in Rotterdam. She trained at the University of Groningen and has since written regularly on nineteenth- and twentieth-century architecture, urban planning and public housing. She has written several books, including a monograph on S.J. van Embden in the Monographs series on Dutch urban planners commissioned by the Netherlands Institute for Spatial Planning and Housing. She recently published the *Architectuurgids Breda and Heerlen, Architectuur en Stedenbouw 1850-1940*.

Hans Ibelings is an architecture historian and author of various books, including *20th Century Architecture in the Netherlands, Supermodernism: Architecture in the Age og Globalization* and monographs on Claus en Kaan, Meyer & Van Schooten, Van Herk & De Kleijn.

Marieke Kuipers is a professor of cultural heritage at the University of Maastricht as well as a senior staff member in cultural value research at the Netherlands Department for Conservation. She writes regularly on 'new monuments' in the Netherlands and abroad. In 1987 she was awarded a doctorate for her thesis *Bouwen in beton, experimenten in de volkshuisvesting voor 1940*, and she edited *Toonbeelden van de wederopbouw. Architectuur, stedenbouw en landinrichting van herrijzend Nederland* (2002).

Ellen Smit is an architecture historian and works as a curator of the maquette collection at the Netherlands Architecture Institute (NAI) in Rotterdam.

Vladimir Stissi is affiliated with the University of Amsterdam as an archaeologist and architecture historian and is amongst others president of the Cuypersgenootschap. In recent years he has conducted research into, among other things, the Amsterdam School, housing construction in Amsterdam from 1850 to 1940 and revival styles in the twentieth century. In addition he regularly writes critiques and reviews, for such publications as *Archined*, on old and current architecture.

Marinke Steenhuis concentrates on the application of cultural history research in current spatial planning projects. As a member of the editorial staff of the journal *Blauwe Kamer*, she writes regularly on current urban planning and landscape topics. She is president of the North Holland Provincial Monuments Commission and a member of the city of Breda's Architecture and Urban Planning Commission. Her contribution to this book is an adaptation of a chapter in her thesis on the urban planner P. Verhagen (1882-1950), which she is finalizing at the moment.

Marcel Teunissen is an architecture historian and has been working since 1999 at the Architectuurproducties agency in The Hague, which produced, among others, the publications *Stad in vorm. De vernieuwing van Den Haag 1985-2000* and *Wonen in Den Haag*. Architectuurproducties produced exhibitions, conducts research for various clients and is involved in such infrastructure projects as the HSL-Zuid high-speed railway line and the renovation of the A12 motorway. A monograph on the architect Theo Bosch and a publication and exhibition about the architecture of the Nieuwe Haagse School in the period between the world wars are in preparation.

Martien de Vletter has been working at the Netherlands Architecture Institute (NAI) since 1987. She directed, along with Ed Taverne and Cor Wagenaar, the publication and exhibition on J.J.P. Oud in 2001, and has since put together the exhibitions Uit eigen Huis, UN Studio UN Fold and Tatirama. She has written on architecture and urban planning in the former Dutch East Indies and the first years following the independence of Indonesia. In the summer of 2004 her publication on architecture and urban planning in the 1970s will be published, to accompany an exhibition on the same subject.

Mariet Willinge is an architecture historian and is, since 1988, head of the department Collection of the Netherlands Architecture Institute (NAI). Since 1998, she is Secretary General of the International Confederation of Architectural Museums. Willinge is amongst others co-editor of the publication *Toonbeelden van de Wederopbouw, Architectuur, stedenbouw en landinrichting van herrijzend Nederland* (2002).

This publication coincides with the exhibition *Living in the Lowlands. The Domestic Scene in the NAI Collection* in the Netherlands Architecture Institute, Rotterdam

Compilation
JaapJan Berg *NAI*
Jean-Paul Baeten *NAI*
Véronique Patteeuw *NAi Publishers*

Copy editing
Pierre Bouvier

Translation
Pierre Bouvier, Andrew May

Image research
Christel Leenen

Photography NAI collection
Martien Kerkhof

Cover illustration
M. de Klerk, P. Kramer, Housing complex De Dageraad, P.L. Takstraat area, Amsterdam, 1921-1923, view from the schoolsquare in the direction of the P.L. Takstraat (photo B. Eilers 1924), NAI collection, Tentoonstellingsraad archive

Design
Mevis & Van Deursen

Printing and lithography
Drukkerij Die Keure, Bruges

Printed on
Fastprint Color Crème, 120 grs.
Munken Print 15, 115 grs.
Fastprint Bio Natural, 120 grs.
Munken Print Extra 15, 115 grs.
Signature, 120 grs.

Binding
IBW, Oostkamp

Production
Véronique Patteeuw, *NAi Publishers*

Publisher
Simon Franke, *NAi Publishers*

© NAi Publishers, Rotterdam, 2004

Available in North, South and Central America through D.A.P./Distributed Art Publishers Inc, 155 Sixth Avenue 2nd Floor, New York, NY 10013-1507, Tel 212 6271999, Fax 212 6279484.

Available in the United Kingdom and Ireland through Art Data, 12 Bell Industrial Estate, 50 Cunnington Street, London W4 5HB, Tel 208 7471061, Fax 208 7422319.

NAi Publishers is an internationally orientated publisher specialized in developing, producing and distributing books on architecture, visual arts and related disciplines.

www.naipublishers.nl

ISBN 90-5662-386-9

Printed and bound in Belgium

WITHDRAWN-UNL